geeks who drink
presents

Duh!

geeks who drink
presents

Duh!

100 BAR TRIVIA QUESTIONS YOU SHOULD KNOW

(AND THE UNEXPECTED STORIES BEHIND THE ANSWERS)

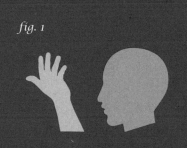

fig. 1

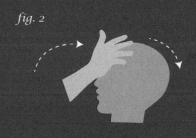

fig. 2

fig. 3

Edited by

CHRISTOPHER D. SHORT

ADAMS MEDIA

NEW YORK   LONDON   TORONTO   SYDNEY   NEW DELHI

Adams Media
An Imprint of Simon & Schuster, Inc.
57 Littlefield Street
Avon, Massachusetts 02322

First Adams Media trade paperback edition September 2019

ADAMS MEDIA and colophon are trademarks of Simon & Schuster.

For information about special discounts for bulk purchases, please contact Simon & Schuster Special Sales at 1-866-506-1949 or business@simonandschuster.com.

The Simon & Schuster Speakers Bureau can bring authors to your live event. For more information or to book an event contact the Simon & Schuster Speakers Bureau at 1-866-248-3049 or visit our website at www.simonspeakers.com.

Interior design by Colleen Cunningham
Interior mug image © 123RF/Agnieszka Murphy

Manufactured in the United States of America

10 9 8 7 6 5 4 3 2 1

Library of Congress Cataloging-in-Publication Data
Names: Short, Christopher D., editor.
Title: Geeks Who Drink presents: Duh! / edited by Christopher D. Short.
Description: Avon, Massachusetts: Adams Media, 2019.
Identifiers: LCCN 2019016953 | ISBN 9781507210499 (pb) | ISBN 9781507210505 (ebook)
Subjects: LCSH: Curiosities and wonders. | Questions and answers. | BISAC: REFERENCE / Trivia. | GAMES / Trivia.
Classification: LCC AG243 .G36 2019 | DDC 031.02--dc23
LC record available at https://lccn.loc.gov/2019016953

ISBN 978-1-5072-1049-9
ISBN 978-1-5072-1050-5 (ebook)

Contents

Introduction 13

 1 CREATING DIVERSIONS 15

2 JOCK SCRAPS

3 EAT ME! 73

In January 2011, *High Times* magazine put out a special edition to celebrate what issue number? 103

The Diorama bag is made by what French fashion house? 105

In the McDonaldland ads, Captain Crook was singularly obsessed with stealing what sandwich? 107

Olive oil and palm oil were the original main ingredients of what soap brand? 110

SJP Collection is a shoe and handbag line created by what actress? 112

Archer Farms is a house brand sold by what retail giant? 114

The world's biggest jetliner, the *A380*, is a product of what company? 117

A guy saw his sister Mabel make mascara out of Vaseline and went on to found what company? 119

What company built the Italian Automobile Factory in Turin? 121

Earl Silas Tupper is best known as the inventor of what product? 123

Dr. Klaus Märtens is best known for what occupation? 125

The Starbucks siren's crown is adorned with what symbol? 127

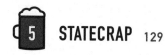 **5 STATECRAP** 129

6 A WORLD OF PAIN 153

7 UH-OH, IT'S A SCIENCE CHAPTER 183

8 IT'S LIT 207

Geeks Who Drink Presents: Duh!

Introduction

- **What's the name of a female peacock?**

- **There are two X's in the logo of what beer brand?**

- **What's the only state flag that depicts a US president?**

These questions are ridiculously obvious, right? You *should* be able to spit out the answer in no time flat? Or...maybe not?

Let's back up a minute. The *usual* job of the conscientious quiz-writer is to start with a kernel of something you don't know, and stir in just the right mix of hints and parallels to lead you to the correct answer (yes, no matter what it feels like, we *do* want you to get most of them right).

You won't find those types of questions here. *Geeks Who Drink Presents: Duh!* starts with one hundred especially super-obvious questions to which, on some level or another, you really should just *know* the answer. Maybe that answer's on the tip of your tongue. Maybe it really wants to get out, but you can't believe it's that straightforward. Anyway, hinting would just ruin it. These questions are carefully crafted so as to dare you to overthink them. You may get it right or not, but when you see the answer, you'll definitely go, "Duh!"

Why would we do this to you? Well, long before we grew into a coast-to-coast pub quiz empire, back in the day when Tobey Maguire was still Spider-Man and Sarah Palin was still a governor, Geeks Who Drink was just a few people trying to find clever ways to ask questions—eight questions a round, eight rounds a quiz, six quizzes a week—that didn't sound like they came right off a Trivial Pursuit card. Those three gems above became the germ of our favorite round theme, and it had legs: as of this writing, more than a decade later, we've presented some 860 Duh questions.

And we've used one hundred of our favorites as jumping-off points for the essays in this book, so let's talk about that real quick! Start by looking through the Table of Contents (duh), where you'll find one hundred questions with corresponding page numbers. Turn 'em over in your brain for a minute, and when you're done torturing yourself over a question, just flip to that page. You'll not only alleviate your suffering; you'll also be treated with a nice little not-so-deep dive into the pool of random knowledge that our writers wade in every day. Speaking of those writers, the initials at the end of each entry just tell you which of our lovely and talented contributors wrote it. You can learn more about them at the back, so please do!

And with that, go forth and enjoy the book. As for us, we're proud as a **peahen**, and ready to enjoy a nice **Dos Equis** in **Washington** (duh).

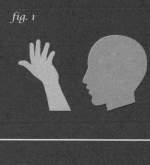

fig. 1

fig. 2

fig. 3

1

CREATING

DIVERSIONS

Q. What's the first round of *Jeopardy!* called?

A. "Jeopardy!"

What more is there to say about the last show standing from the golden age of TV quizzes? With its lightning pace and trademark twist on responses—"*form of a question*," you have likely yelled in your living room—*Jeopardy!* holds a special place in the hearts of game show nerds and dining grandparents everywhere.

Created by Merv Griffin while on a plane with his wife, in a story that's not interesting enough to be repeated as often as it is, *Jeopardy!* has aired more than eleven thousand episodes in various iterations since its first bow on NBC in the mid-sixties. The "newest" version, with sometimes-snarky septuagenarian Alex Trebek, has been a syndicated stalwart since 1984.

Despite a reputation for strict rules that occasionally border on pedantry, the *Jeopardy!* staff are not exactly the grammar police.[1] As the lore goes, Griffin originally meant to require "grammatically correct phrasing" (for example, only accepting "Who is" when the subject is a person). But this slowed the game down, and the rules were changed to accept any correct response in question form. Nowadays, "Where is Duh?" is a perfectly valid response to a clue about this book. And if you really want to be cool, by *Jeopardy!* standards anyway, try to remember that you don't need a "What is" in front of *Who's Afraid of Virginia Woolf?*—it's already a question.

When young people notice *Jeopardy!* at all, that generally means there's a new viral video of some hiccup, embarrassing moment, or other bizarre occurrence:

---

1. The rest of the rules aren't that draconian either. As long as you pronounce the answer in a way that's phonetically feasible, you're golden.

- In November 2018 a contestant named Myra signaled quickly[2] to carry on the rich tradition of Jeopardistas who suck at pop culture. Mortifyingly, she mistook a photo of sad white rap-rocker Uncle Kracker for the way more talented, way more melanated rapper Kid Cudi.
- There's practically a whole *YouTube* genre of players swinging and missing on sports questions. One contestant placed "running back Marcus Allen" on the Colorado Rockies. Another named Magic Johnson as the all-time NHL assists leader. In February 2018 all three players stood and stared as an entire elementary football category went by—they didn't even get "option play" when they spotted the word "choice."
- At the 2011 Tournament of Champions, Kara Spak memorably provoked Trebek to question her background by guessing, "What is a threesome?"[3] The correct response to that clue, given on the rebound by eventual champion Roger Craig: "What is a love triangle?"

For the record, although the second round is called "Double Jeopardy!"—a play on the Fifth Amendment clause that protects you from being tried twice on the same charges—the first round of *Jeopardy!* is not called "Single Jeopardy." It's just "Jeopardy!"

Or—again, this would be a valid, if obnoxious, response—"What's the deal with *Jeopardy!*?"

—N.H.

2. Not "buzzed in." Trebek always says "pick up your signaling devices," because there isn't actually a buzzing sound when players…um, buzz in. See also the constant lectern/podium debate. Believe us, *Jeopardy!* fans get testy about some weird, random shit.

3. The clue: "If Andy yearns for Brenda, and Brenda cares about Charlene, who pines for Andy, the three of them form one of these." And if Spak's name sounds familiar, that might be because she's one of the four *Jeopardy!* champions whose work appears elsewhere in this book. Thus ends our plug for the bio page!

Q. Tracey Ullman was introduced to America on what show?

A. The Tracey Ullman Show.

At the end of each episode of *The Tracey Ullman Show*, broadcast on the fledgling Fox network from 1987 to 1990, Ullman dismissed her studio audience with the catchphrase "Go home!" She later said she couldn't think of anything funnier to say—this, from the woman who backed herself out of a professional ballet career as a teenager, after forgetting to wear underwear for a performance.[1]

Ullman landed right-side up and recovered, churning out comedy gold on both sides of the Atlantic. Probably the best-known British female comic stateside,[2] she's also the richest in her native England. But it wasn't always that way; her greatest contribution to pop culture netted her practically nothing.

The longest-running scripted show in American TV history, *The Simpsons* started with creator Matt Groening's quirky between-segment vignettes on *Tracey Ullman*. "I breastfed those little devils," Ullman quipped at the 1990 Emmys ceremony. Indeed, during the first week of filming, producer James L. Brooks needed actors to voice the Simpson family, and *Tracey Ullman* cast members Dan Castellaneta, Julie Kavner, Nancy Cartwright, and Yeardley Smith stepped up. Smash cut to 2008, when their salaries topped out at $400,000 per episode.

---

1. In a stand-up special, Ullman spoke about that fateful day: "As we twirled and snapped our fingers, I felt light and airy and fancy-free. Of course I did, I had no *bloody panties on*! And the cartwheel lift's coming up! And I'm a brunette!"

2. After *The Tracey Ullman Show*, she starred in *Tracey Takes On...*, *Tracey Ullman in the Trailer Tales*, *Tracey Ullman's State of the Union*, *Tracey Breaks the News*, and *Tracey Ullman's Show*. It's never hard to tell who's in her stuff.

Ullman herself didn't voice anyone, and with none of that *Simpsons* cash coming her way, she sued Fox for $2.25 million worth of merchandising—this was in 1991, mind you, roughly eighteen months after *The Simpsons* debuted as its own thing, so no one had any idea those sales would reach $4.6 *billion* by 2014. Not that it would have mattered anyway: she *also* didn't create the characters, so she lost the suit.

But by forging her reputation as a walking solo *Saturday Night Live*, Ullman did at least win Fox its first two Emmys and set the network on a course toward a sort of non-*Simpsons* niche. A parade of well-received early-nineties Fox sketch shows may not have burned up the ratings, but they did force *SNL* to wake up from its 1980s stupor:

- Critically acclaimed, Emmy-winning ratings flop ***The Ben Stiller Show***, which began in 1992, was canceled after thirteen episodes. In the meantime, it helped launch the careers of Stiller, Andy Dick, Janeane Garofalo, Bob Odenkirk, and Judd Apatow. Not bad![3]
- Best known for giving us J.Lo, Jim Carrey, Jamie Foxx, and the various Wayanses, ***In Living Color*** also forced the NFL to up its game. In 1992, they lured some twenty million viewers away from CBS to watch a live episode during the Super Bowl's lame halftime ice-dancing show. In 1993, the Super Bowl got Michael Jackson.
- You're somewhat less likely to remember ***The Edge***, which ran from 1992 to 1993, but if nothing else it should be deeply appreciated for *not* launching Jennifer Aniston's sketch-comedy career.

—L.C.

---

3. Stiller had already peaced out from *SNL* after just four episodes in 1989. MTV then recruited him to create its first non-music show, which was canceled after one season, leading to the ill-fated Fox show. Where do you think he learned to play a sad sack?

Q. Peter Gabriel's first three albums all had what two-word title?

A. Peter Gabriel.

In November 1974, Genesis was one week into the ultra-complicated concert tour that followed its ultra-complicated double album, *The Lamb Lies Down on Broadway*, when front man and cofounder Peter Gabriel told his bandmates that he'd leave the group after the tour. He dutifully wore his lumpen latex "Slipperman" costume[1] for another ninety-nine tour dates and then announced his departure in a letter that he sent to the British press the following August.

"I felt I should look at/learn about/develop myself," he wrote. "It was important to me to give space to my family, which I wanted to hold together, and to liberate the daddy in me."

Eleven months after he delivered the letter—and forced everyone to read the phrase "liberate the daddy in me"—Gabriel started working on his first solo record, which he called...*Peter Gabriel*. It reached number seven on the UK charts, gave us the almost literally inescapably catchy "Solsbury Hill," and inspired him to record a quick follow-up called... *Peter Gabriel*.

"I tried to do a lot of things to separate me from Genesis," he told a British magazine in 2007. "It took me until album number three before I found an identity." That third album was called... Well, let's just say Gabriel's long-awaited "identity" seemed to be "Peter Gabriel." But in 1982, when he named his fourth solo effort *Peter Gabriel*, Geffen Records

---

1. If you're thinking about Googling this, we strongly recommend that you not.

executives slapped its plastic wrap with stickers that read "Security," a name it's gone by semi-officially, especially in America, ever since.[2]

Mind you, Gabriel isn't the only artist who can't be bothered to title an album:

- As of this writing, Weezer has six albums called **Weezer**, which are distinguished from each other by the colors of their covers, starting with their debut "Blue Album" in 1994. Debating how many of them are any good at all, though a favorite pastime of ours, is sadly beyond the scope of this book.
- Twenty-three of the thirty-six studio, live, and compilation records by enduring soft-rockers Chicago are called **Chicago**. They're currently up to *Chicago XXXVI*, because apparently the band that did "You're the Inspiration" have decided they're too fancy for regular Arabic numerals.
- The King of Latin Music is also the King of Un-Googleable Records: the lengthy discography of Brazilian singer-songwriter Roberto Carlos includes thirty-seven albums called **Roberto Carlos** (and one named **Roberto Carlos Remixed**). *Uau!*

After *Security*, it took Gabriel four years to put out his next solo record. Barred from using his name again, he picked an "anti-title," which worked out pretty well: *So* garnered an Album of the Year Grammy nomination, spawned his only ever number-one single on the Billboard Hot 100,[3]

---

2. Thanks to their different cover art, fans call the first three albums *Car*, *Scratch*, and *Melt*, respectively. Incidentally, Gabriel recorded German-language versions of *Melt* and *Security*, called *Ein Deutsches Album* ("A German Album") and *Deutsches Album* ("German Album" without the "a"). Dude, *was zur Hölle?*

3. As this was the zenith of the pretentious world-beat craze, the album lost to Paul Simon's *Graceland*. Gabriel's chart-topping single, "Sledgehammer," featured the immortal line "Open up your fruit cage, where the fruit is as sweet as can be." Future historians will agree that there was never a sillier year than 1986.

and sold five million copies in the US alone. And when *The Daily Mail* cover-mounted his greatest hits onto a Sunday edition in 2007, that disc included four tracks from *So*.

The title of the compilation? *Peter Gabriel.*

—J.C.

Q. Composer John Philip Sousa died in what month?

Ancient Romans called the third month Martius to honor the surly war god Mars, father of mythic city-founder Romulus. Mars also gave us the word *martial*—but not the walking/musical term *march*, which ultimately goes back to Old High German. But we'd never let such hairsplitting rob you of a biography!

Known even in his lifetime as "The March King," John Philip Sousa did indeed compose more than 130 marches—"The Stars and Stripes Forever" is America's national march, and the "Freebird" of high school half-time shows. He also finished around fifteen operettas, eleven waltzes, and an actual bestselling novel.[1]

Born in DC in 1854, a thirteen-year-old Sousa was overheard practicing by a passing-by circus bandleader, who invited him to leave home and join up.[2] He totally would've done it, too, had his dad not caught wind of the scheme and forcibly enlisted him in the Marine Corps instead. Crisis averted!

Our hero would stay in the service for nineteen of his next twenty-four years, conducting the Marine Band from 1880, and molding it into Washington's top ensemble. In 1890, recording some of its greatest hits for the

---

1. A virtuoso tries to trade his soul for Satan's magic fiddle in *The Fifth String*—published some thirty years before Charlie Daniels was even born.

2. Child musician-soldiers were pretty common in America back then. During the Civil War, ten-year-old John Clem was an unofficial drummer boy/mascot for the 22nd Michigan Regiment. Some accounts say he fought at the Battle of Chickamauga using a sawed-off musket, which has forced us to coin the word *horridorable*.

nascent phonograph, the band made J.P. one of America's first pop stars. The middle-aged Sousa worried that this newfangled "canned music" would kill creativity and weaken "the national throat," whatever that means.

Nonetheless, he took advantage of the success and led the Marine Band on its first national tour in 1891 (they still do it annually to this day). After the second tour netted him a head-turning $8,000—some 225 grand in 2019 dollars—Sousa stepped down to organize a civilian band that somehow played more than fifteen thousand shows over the next four decades.[3] It's hardly surprising, then, that Sousa died of heart failure on March 6, 1932.

Besides the tunes you hear wherever two or more brass players are gathered, Sousa left some other enduring legacies:

- In 1893 he commissioned a more-portable version of the tuba, whose sound would "diffuse over the entire band like the frosting on a cake!" Pleased with the curlicued curiosity, a sanguine Sousa predicted every American home would someday own a sousaphone.
- The Sousa Bridge carries Pennsylvania Avenue over the Anacostia, southeast of the Capitol and not far from John's birthplace. Two prior bridges had burned down there—one on purpose, to stymie the Brits in the War of 1812, and another when the steam stack of a passing ship got jammed in it. But brooking no nonsense even in death, Sousa has kept *his* bridge standing ramrod-straight since 1940.
- John Philip Sousa IV founded a Tea Party fundraising group called—what else?—the Stars & Stripes Forever PAC. He raised more than $7 million for the 2016 presidential run of Ben Carson, who proceeded to advocate the selection of Supreme Court justices by looking at "the fruit salad of their life."

—E.K.

---

3. For comparison's sake, the Rolling Stones have yet to crack the three thousand mark, despite access to much stronger amphetamines.

Q. *Millipede* was the sequel to what classic 1981 arcade game?

A. Centipede.

Regarded as one of history's greatest games, *Centipede* was at the back end of the early wave of arcade hits that included *Space Invaders*, *Galaxian*, and *Asteroids*. Players controlled a "bug blaster," firing lasers at a centipede that dropped down the vertical screen through a labyrinth of mushroom caps. Fleas, spiders, and other bugs showed up occasionally to try and destroy the bug blaster. It made as much sense as any video game, really.

Centipede was the first game to use Atari's 2.5-inch trackball,[1] and a rare title with a female cocreator, Dona Bailey.[2] An immediate huge success by any measure, it was also one of the first arcade games to attract a large female player base, and you can still play it today, in various retro gaming packs and at revival arcades.

Released in 1982, *Millipede* was already in the works before they knew *Centipede* had legs.[3] Instead of a "blaster," the player is represented by a large arrow, which shoots smaller arrows into a field of mushrooms, flowers,

1. Invented by British engineer Ralph Benjamin in the 1940s, trackballs were first used by the Royal Canadian Navy as part of a digital radar system. They mounted a standard Canadian five-pin bowling ball on a set of air rollers and connected disks, which in turn were connected to a series of shipboard sensors. Almost as much fun as *Golden Tee Golf*!

2. Other notable women in those early days: Carol Shaw, who developed a 3-D computer version of Tic-Tac-Toe in 1978; Roberta Williams, the cofounder of Sierra On-Line and creator of the King's Quest series; and Brenda Romero, who developed an early online role-playing game called *Wizardry*, as well as a *Sims*-like game set in the Playboy Mansion of all places. That might be all of them; the industry has never been great that way. Even Bailey bailed from Atari before *Millipede*.

3. See what we did there?

and bugs. The arrow, apparently, represents an archer, the son of a dead, disgraced king, whose evil spirit has unleashed a plague of insects. It...well, it kind of makes less sense than *Centipede*, right?

It may not have reached the heights of its predecessor, but *Millipede* is in no danger of inclusion among the Worst Video Game Sequels of All Time:

- **Pac-Man 2: The New Adventures.** A bizarre quest game from 1994, this Sega Genesis title follows Namco's yellow blob as he runs errands for his family: obtaining milk for Pac-Baby, trolleying to the mountains to get a flower for Pac Jr.'s girlfriend, and fighting a Gum Monster created by a Ghost Witch. As one does.
- **Super Mario Bros. 2.** A rare misfire in the otherwise unimpeachable series, this quick cash-in reskinned characters from the unrelated Japanese game *Doki Doki Panic*, and tried to fool players into thinking they'd returned to Mario World via the old "dream world" trope. Pluck your own damn turnips, Nintendo!
- **Duke Nukem Forever.** Announced in 1998, released in 2011, this sequel to a beloved early-era first-person shooter featured shoddy mechanics, glitchy animation, and outdated gross-out humor, including abortion jokes and the ability to throw poop at enemies.

Nor was *Millipede* the last chapter of the *Centipede* story; in 2011, a run-and-gun reboot called *Centipede: Infestation* appeared on Nintendo's Wii and 3DS systems. Its bizarre post-apocalyptic storyline starred anime-style tweens named Max and Maisy, who spouted corny dialogue and exhibited age-inappropriate sexual tension. Critics mostly ignored it, but *YouTube* videos make it look, you know, pretty fun.

Hey, it's hard to mess up bug blasting!

—N.P.

Q. In *The Shawshank Redemption*, Andy hid his rock hammer by cutting into which book of the Bible?

A. Exodus.

If you subscribe to the "write what you know" school of creativity, then it makes perfect sense that lifelong Mainer Stephen King likes to fill in details with stuff he can see from the veranda of his old creepy Bangor mansion. Starting with his debut novel, 1974's *Carrie*, his Maine-a-lo-mania was still going strong when he set his 1982 novella "Rita Hayworth and the Shawshank Redemption" at a fictional prison in the "Pine Tree State."[1]

Thought by King himself to be unfilmable, the one-long-flashback tale nonetheless caught the attention of Frank Darabont, a screenwriter whose biggest splash at that point was *A Nightmare on Elm Street 3*.[2] He picked up the rights in 1989 for $5,000, worked it into a tear-jerky script—and somehow managed to get into the director's chair, too, even though that column of his resume was even thinner.

With its title not truncated quite enough for befuddled audiences, *The Shawshank Redemption* grossed just $16 million at the box office in 1994, against a $25 million budget (it also didn't help that it was competing against *Forrest Gump* and *Pulp Fiction*). Needless to say, it picked up momentum from there: nominated for seven Oscars (but winning none), its award-season rerelease got the movie to break even. Then it became a sleeper hit on home video, becoming the number-one rental of 1995.

1. "Write what you know" doesn't apply to the prison stuff. King did get arrested once, in 1970, for stealing traffic cones, but he only had to pay a $100 fine.

2. Roger Ebert hailed it as "a machine-made script...devised as a series of pegs to hang the special effects on."

Before all that, though, TV magnate Ted Turner had bought *Shawshank*'s production company, Castle Rock Entertainment,[3] also picking up the rights to *City Slickers*, *When Harry Met Sally...*, and a not-yet-number-one sitcom called *Seinfeld*. Depending on which legend you believe, at least one of three factors might have put *Shawshank* over:

- The licensing fee was based on box-office receipts, so it was a classic buy-low scenario.
- Part of the acquisition deal stipulated that Turner could show all Castle Rock properties as often as he liked.
- He straight-up sold himself the rights at a Castle Rock–bottom price.

Whatever the reason, Turner turned TNT into the *Shawshank* channel, even more than he turned TBS into the *Beastmaster* station—which was so much that "The Beastmaster Station" was actually a contemporary joke. With its extra-long run time, the *Shawshank* broadcast can sneak more commercials around the third-act escape scenes, and we will all happily sit through them; indeed, *IMDb* users have long since decided it is the very best film of all time.

Getting back to the original subject: symbolism aside, if you want to hide a rock hammer in a hollowed-out Bible, we recommend starting a bit further back. Exodus is just a few pages into the notoriously thick holy text, so you're begging to be found out. If you start in Joshua instead, you can cut out all that Canaanite genocide, while still retaining the sexy parts of Deuteronomy. Happy digging!

—J.T.

---

3. Named for the fictional setting of several King stories, including "The Body." Rob Reiner picked that name for his production company because he'd had so much success with the adaptation *Stand by Me*, also the best movie ever to feature a crowd chanting "Lardass." Coincidentally, "Shawshank" and "The Body" are both in the same short-story collection, *Different Seasons*.

Q. "Whose dish is on the chopping block?" So goes a catchphrase from what reality competition?

A. Chopped.

For more than a decade, Ted Allen has been posing this question to culinary saps, who willingly test their cooking skills and mental health on this Food Network fixture.

As Allen himself is fond of recounting to journalists, albeit with a distinct apocryphal haze, the show started with a weird and tragically unaired pilot. Set in a mansion, it was hosted by a butler character, who would summon the contestants in limos, and then feed the losing dish to his Beverly Hills Chihuahua.[1] That host was *not* Ted Allen; as part of their streamlining the pitch into a workable show, the Food Network wisely decided to bring in the affable food and wine expert from *Queer Eye for the Straight Guy*, and a franchise was born.[2]

Four chefs—ranging from unappreciated line cook to executive chef with delusions of grandeur—are presented with four bizarrely disparate ingredients in a "mystery basket." They have 20 minutes to cook an appetizer, and then 30 minutes each to churn out an entree and dessert. In that time frame, they must complete four edible portions—no blood, no cross-contamination, no raw chicken, no death.[3] Three plates go to the

1. It probably would have worked better if they fed the losing *contestant* to the Chihuahua. Think of the ratings!

2. And a franchise it is. So far, it has spawned such spinoffs as *Chopped Junior*, *Chopped All-Stars*, *Chopped Grill Masters*, and *Chopped After Hours*—and that's just in the US. Sadly, though, *Chopped South Africa* went the way of the Chihuahua after just two seasons.

3. In 450-plus episodes, three of those four things have happened at least once. In the season twenty-eight "Deadliest Baskets" episode, one contestant was axed for serving the judges a whole, but poisonous-if-crushed, Andean cherimoya seed.

professional chef judges, who decide whether the contestant moved them to tears of joy or disgust with their Fruity Pebble–encrusted sea bass. The fourth plate lives under a *cloche*, over which Allen pauses dramatically while he trots out the catchphrase before throwing to commercial (to make sure you don't change the channel, natch).

By the way, don't think we're not going to explain what "bizarrely disparate" means:

- In season four, one dessert basket featured tofu skins, star fruit, avocados, and oyster sauce. The episode winner, Michael Siry, made avocado spring rolls with caramel oyster dipping sauce. Sounds delicious, but judge Aarón Sánchez dinged him for using the star fruit as a boring old garnish.
- The entree basket for a season twenty-one "Ultimate Champions" episode had a rack of lamb, papayas, spring garlic, and…Peppermint Patties. As winner Diana Sabater said in a recap, "I wanted to shave off the chocolate and just use the peppermint with the lamb, but there was no way for me to cut the chocolate off." If we had a nickel for every time *that* happened…
- *Chopped* has amped up the weird in recent years by including sketchy global foods. The season twenty-two "Bizarre Baskets" episode— judged by *Bizarre Foods* host Andrew Zimmern—included chopped camel, a Russian meat gel called *kholodets*, and a Turkish shredded-chicken dessert pudding called *tavuk göğsü*. We'd look up what the chefs made from that, but we're busy making sure our own dinner stays down.

—L.C.

Q. Porky's cartoon girlfriend Petunia has most often worn what hairstyle?

A. Pigtails.

In point of fact, Petunia Pig had no hair at all when she was spawned from the proverbial (delicious) rib of that curiously similar-looking male character.[1] For that matter, the Warner Bros. animators have generally ignored her altogether: after five Porky shorts in the 1930s (she finally got her pigtails in the fourth), Petunia vanished from the *Looney Tunes* cast for decades. After a couple of appearances in specials of the seventies and eighties, she only came back for *real* in the third millennium, with Cartoon Network's *Baby Looney Tunes*[2]—sure enough, still sporting her pun-tastic signature 'do.

Before those tied-off hair clumps, the word "pigtail" had to take a detour through the American South. From the seventeenth century, farmers used it to refer to twisted-up rolls of tobacco leaves—apparently perfect for cutting off and chewing—which did indeed look like those famous corkscrew tails. Since then, pigtail tobacco has never totally gone away, any more than tobacco chewing itself has: Meriwether Lewis bought 130 rolls for his 1803 excursion with William Clark; Jim found some in *Treasure Island* while going through Billy Bones's pockets; and it's still sold that way sometimes by specialty tobacconists.[3]

1. See also: Minnie Mouse, Daisy Duck, Penelope Pussycat, Winnie Woodpecker, Smurfette, the Chipettes, the Tasmanian She-Devil, and every single female S.O. in *Bambi*: Faline, Bluebelle, and that rabbit who is seriously known only as "Thumper's wife."

2. Yes, maybe it was a blatant rip-off of *Muppet Babies*, but it was also the only Looney project ever in which Petunia got her own Porky-free storylines. #SowPower

3. Just look for that thing that resembles a faceless poop emoji. Delicious!

It was around 1750 that sailors finally started using "pigtail" to refer to their dude-ponies. Since then, whether braided or unbraided, single or in pairs, folks have been tying their hair back and comparing it to that handy ham handle. Some other pigtail aficionados of fact and fiction:

- After the fall of the Qing dynasty in 1912, General Zhang Xun chose to keep his single braid, called the "queue," even though it wasn't compulsory anymore. It wasn't his last act that reminds us of hair—in 1917 he led the failed Manchu Restoration that would have restored monarchy to China.
- The 1960s saw a mini-boom in the hairstyle, as Gilligan's Islander Mary Ann Summers and Beverly Hillbilly Elly May Clampett both rocked the farmer's-daughter look. Donna Douglas, who played the latter, successfully settled out of court in 2011 after Mattel made an Elly May Barbie doll without her permission. One might even say Mattel were the *sue-ees*.
- While British judges' wigs are traditionally long and rug-like all around the head, the famous barrister wigs have low foreheads and pigtails. Supposedly they give the wearers a degree of anonymity, so they can prosecute dangerous criminals without, you know, something bad happening to those nice kneecaps of theirs.

As for Petunia? *Baby Looney Tunes* went off the air in 2005. Ten years later, when Cartoon Network did yet another franchise retread called *New Looney Tunes*, Petunia got a second makeover: she now wears a loose bob with bangs and a single bow. The pigtails may be gone, but she's still looking swine!

—L.M.P.

Q. The narration on *Gossip Girl* was provided by what character?

A. Gossip Girl.

"Gossip Girl here, your one and only source into the scandalous lives of Manhattan's elite." So started each of the 121 TV episodes, over six seasons of drug-, drama-, and sex-fueled coming-of-age stories. Based on the bestselling young-adult novels by Cecily von Ziegesar, herself a graduate of Manhattan's exclusive Nightingale-Bamford School, *Gossip Girl* followed the antics of the impeccably named blue-blood characters Serena van der Woodsen, Blair Waldorf, Nathaniel Archibald, and Charles "Chuck" Bass.

The mysteriously omniscient title character was an anonymous blogger—in the early days of when there was even such a thing as a "blogger" (the series ran from 2007 to 2012). And if Gossip Girl's narration sounds familiar, that's because she was voiced by Kristen Bell, also the title star of The CW's voiceover-heavy *Veronica Mars*.[1]

While it wasn't the most-watched show on TV,[2] *Gossip Girl* did foretell and even influence the future in a few ways:

- Popularizing streaming episodes. New *Gossip Girl* shows were often the most downloaded on iTunes—and sure, "downloaded

1. If that's still not ringing a bell (so to speak), Kristen's voice has been *all over the place* since then. She's the voice of Anna in *Frozen*, Priscilla the sloth in *Zootopia,* and Jade in *Teen Titans Go! To the Movies*. If you've never been around a child or teen, just watch her on *The Good Place*, I guess.

2. In fact, it never rose above number 135 in the ratings for a full season. Why? Um, we'll bet you a dollar that even now you can't name your local CW affiliate without looking.

on iTunes" sounds antiquated *now*, but do remember that Netflix didn't even start its streaming service until 2007, the same year we found out what a Leighton Meester is.

- Launching obsessive TV recaps. If it's hard to imagine waking up on a Monday and not reading about last night's *Game of Thrones*, you can thank Blake Lively's lip gloss. Every moment, every scene, every filming location, and who was dating who on the show versus real life: all of it was recounted by bloggers. It was oh so meta.
- Showing us how awful we are. The very structure of the show predicted that anonymous scrutiny on blogs and social media would take over our lives, forever changing interactions among teenagers (and adults and children). Yes, we're talking about your finsta.[3]

In the final episode, Gossip Girl was revealed to be sensitive Brooklynite Dan Humphrey—the ultimate lower-class outsider, living in a suspiciously big and nice Brooklyn loft apartment, trying to process his journey through the rarefied social circles of the Upper East Side. Even though it's official canon, fans are still griping about the bogus revelation.

Oh hey—that's another way the show was ahead of its time!

—K.S.

---

3. i.e., a fake *Instagram* account, sometimes used to anonymously post pictures, memes, and criticism of your fellow junior high students. If you have a "finsta," you probably have a "rinsta," or regular *Instagram* account—i.e., the one your parents are supposedly monitoring. Also, you should stop being so sketchy. Just saying.

Q. How old do you need to be to play blackjack in Las Vegas?

Like our memories of stumbling out of the casino those many nights, the origins of blackjack are hazy. Ancient Romans played a counting game with wooden dice, making it the earliest-known distant relative—but we don't know the exact rules of that game.[1] Miguel de Cervantes's 1613 novella "Rinconete y Cortadillo" documented a game called *veintiuna*, and eighteenth-century French casinos offered *vingt-et-un*. As you astute and worldly readers are already aware, both of those things mean "twenty-one."

Gambling reached the Americas big-time when people in French colonial New Orleans played *poque*, which—maybe you guessed this too—is more like poker. The game spread to cities all along the Mississippi, especially aided by the invention of the steamboat, just four years after the nascent United States acquired the river in the Louisiana Purchase. Even though gambling was banned on the mainland, many states somehow found themselves cool with the riverboat kind, and a stereotype was born.

But Twenty-One specifically didn't catch on in the States until 1931, the year Nevada legalized gambling. To sweeten the pot, some Las Vegas casinos offered a special promotion, in which your bet would pay 10-1 if you caught an ace of spades and a jack of either spades or clubs, i.e., a black jack.[2] "That

1. Perhaps they were lost when Jesus flipped over that table.

2. This rule is long gone, but many systems have been devised for gaining an edge in blackjack, most involving complicated mental tabulations. In the 1960s, Edward Thorp became a bestselling author with a card-counting system so easy you can do it on your fingers—though the pit boss will certainly notice that and have you thrown out. In fact, Thorp *did* get banned from many casinos while testing his system, but he literally sneaked back in with fake mustaches and glasses. Classic!

Geeks Who Drink Presents: Duh!

would be a catchy name for the whole game," someone thought, and they weren't wrong. It is still a bit confusing though: any ten-point card can go with an ace to make a blackjack (which now only pays 1.5x).

So why can't you play at eighteen? The short answer is, Nevada doesn't have time for ID juggling. Vegas is basically soaked with booze at all times, especially at gaming tables; if you were an eighteen-year-old gambler, it would cause extra hassle while they tried to remember who was allowed to drink.

Anyway, arbitrary age restrictions are nothing new:

- In rodeo's literal mini-game called mutton busting, kids usually must be between ages four and seven, and under 60 pounds. After all, we wouldn't want to be cruel to the sheep we're riding on.
- In 2016, Hawaii became the first state to raise the smoking age to twenty-one. As of this writing, the state legislature—in a round-about way of banning it altogether—is considering another raise, to age one hundred. The law would go into effect in 2024, so someone born on the day of Hawaii's statehood would still have to wait thirty-five years to burn one. Of course, if you're celebrating *two* centennials, the people around you shouldn't be too judgy.
- The Mars candy company got so tired of child-marketing accusations that now you literally have to verify your age while visiting the M&M's website.[3] Those under thirteen get redirected to a lecture about their marketing standards. It isn't even candy-coated!

—J.T.

---

3. In case you thought of that *other* kind of age-gated website: yes, there is M&M's porn. Now you have to know that.

Q. You can hear Brian Wilson's dogs barking on what Beach Boys album?

The Wilson brothers—Brian, Carl, and Dennis—were sunnily harmonizing in their shared childhood bedroom long before they went pro. Along with cousin Mike Love, they recorded "Surfin'" in 1961, using food money their parents left behind while they were out of town. They dubbed themselves The Pendletones, after a dorky-but-popular flannel shirt of the time. Someone at the record company wisely went ahead and changed it for them.

Five years later, at the ripe age of twenty-four, Brian was all surf-rocked out and getting inspiration from The Beatles' *Rubber Soul*—all the way down to the prodigious LSD consumption. Naturally, he packed *Pet Sounds* with introspective lyrics, crisscrossing harmonies, and the universally beloved squonk of the accordion. Notable numbers included:

- **The instrumental title track**, meant for a James Bond theme. It would've been great for 1967's *You Only Live Twice*—calypso is just the thing for fighting ninjas in a volcano lair.
- **"Sloop John B,"** based on the Bahamian folk song "The John B Sails." Neither is related to singer Jon B, author of the 1998 booty-call anthem "Are U Still Down,"[1] who surely deserves his own namesake ship.
- The sublimely clingy love song **"God Only Knows."** In the 2013 video game *BioShock Infinite*, a seedy composer in an alt-universe

---

1. Featuring Tupac Shakur's final verses, in which he claimed to be "all weak, baby, but I'm strong in parts." We assume he was talking about his pecs—the dude was ripped.

1912 hears the song through a dimensional rift and claims it for his own, making an even-more-bittersweet barbershop version.

In the closing seconds of *Pet Sounds*, Brian's dogs, Louie and Banana, barked over the sound of a pre-recorded locomotive. The barks sound pretty low-pitched; some dog-speak experts would say that suggests a healthy train-wariness.

Like many all-time greats, *Pet Sounds* didn't make much of a splash at first, peaking at number ten and being met with some especially abstruse reviews. The Who's Pete Townshend said it was "written for a feminine audience." *Melody Maker* asked, "Most progressive pop album ever, or sickly as peanut butter?" Even forty years later, cranky critic Robert Christgau called it a "good record, but a totem." We're still not sure if any of those are disses.

Anyway, The Beach Boys never reached those heights again—though at the end of the 1980s, the tropical-malaise schlock anthem "Kokomo" hit number one for a zombie version of the band, with just two of the original family members. By that point, Dennis had chilled with Charles Manson and drowned in a harbor (on separate occasions). Carl hung on until 1998, dying of cancer shortly after his fifty-first birthday.

Depression and drugs turned Brian into a recluse for decades starting around 1973, though he's been recording and touring again since the mid-nineties.[2] In 2004 he even finished *SMiLE*, the *Pet Sounds* sequel that had been shelved for nearly forty years.[3] Typically, without elaborating, Robert Christgau called it "sui generis Americanism."

—E.K.

2. During that renaissance, Wilson once met Eagles front man Don Henley. On Henley's copy of *Pet Sounds* he wrote, "Thanks for all the great songs." Then, after thinking another moment, he crossed out "great" and wrote "good."

3. To capture the beach atmosphere at home, Wilson had a massive sandbox built in his dining room, and his grand piano dropped in the middle. Naturally, his dogs took frequent advantage of this arrangement—we're still hoping for a trilogy-ender called *Pet Smells*.

Q. Miley Stewart was the onscreen alter ego of what Disney Channel title character?

A. Hannah Montana.

This is a story about one real person and two fake ones. Played by Miley Cyrus, Miley Stewart was a sassy brunette teenager by day; at night, she turned into a sparkly blonde pop star named Hannah Montana.[1] Miley Stewart was the daughter of a successful country singer named Robby Ray—played by Cyrus's real-life father, a successful country singer named *Billy* Ray.[2]

Anyway, this was high-level stuff, in case you can't tell. From 2006 to 2011, the House of Mouse spun comedy gold from the shenanigans the Stewarts got into trying to hide her identities. It immediately became the Disney Channel's highest-rated show; in the whole TV landscape, it was second only to *American Idol* among finicky viewers aged six to fourteen. One second-season episode—with *High School Musical 2* as a lead-in, but still—pulled 10.7 *million* viewers, and was loudly trumpeted as the most-watched basic-cable show ever.

In the middle of the storm was an instantly charismatic star. Cyrus was born Destiny Hope in 1992, a stone's throw from Nashville, Tennessee, and

1. Starting with the show's theme song, "Best of Both Worlds," Hannah consistently delivered catchy songs. "You'll Always Find Your Way Back Home" was cowritten by an already-chart-topping Taylor Swift; on "We've Got the Party with Us," she quartetted with the pre-sexual-awakening Jonas Brothers. "Need a Little Love" featured Sheryl Crow—a well-post-heyday Sheryl Crow, who would soon publish a cookbook called *If It Makes You Healthy*, but still.

2. We're not allowed to reproduce the lyrics of his biggest hit, the 1992 chart-topper "Achy Breaky Heart." We can publish the chords though: in order, in their entirety, they are A major and E major.

nicknamed Miley by her family because she was so, um, "smiley." She first auditioned for the show at age eleven,[3] and was just eighteen when it ended. Having toyed around on soundtrack albums with separating her real-life identity from her character's (and her other character's), she jumped to pop stardom, becoming neither the first nor last Disney star to tread that path:

- In the 1950s, *The Mickey Mouse Club* launched the careers of **Annette Funicello**, who had two top-ten hits, and **Frankie Avalon**, who went all the way to number one with "Venus" and "Why." The pair also headlined a string of "beach party" movies in the sixties; in our head canon, if not reality, they've been in every Old Navy commercial.
- *The All-New Mickey Mouse Club* capped off the 1990s by belching out **Christina Aguilera**, **Britney Spears**, and **Justin Timberlake**… and several "it's complicated" love stories.
- In the twenty-first century, *Camp Rock*'s **Demi Lovato** and *Wizards of Waverly Place* star **Selena Gomez** have hit the US top ten a total of ten times. And yet another *Mickey Mouse Club* revival started streaming in 2017, so, you know, brace yourself.

After peaking at number two with "Party in the U.S.A." and "We Can't Stop," Miley finally hit the top exactly once, as of this writing, with the 2013 jam "Wrecking Ball." Its viral nude-trapeze video served as the perfect chaser to that summer's MTV Video Music Awards appearance, where she was crotch-grabbing and grinding on that "Blurred Lines" guy.

We're not sure there's a straight line to be drawn from her tweenage Disney audition to all that stuff. But after all, she *did* get famous leading a double…er, triple life.

—L.C.

---

3. Her dad also had to audition, to play her dad.

Q. The second-eldest Marx Brother played what stringed instrument?

A. Harp.

Unlike the Doobies, Jungles, and Righteouses, the Marx Brothers were real-life siblings. Born in France, their father, "Frenchie," started the family tradition of on-the-nose nicknames involving long vowel sounds. After moving to New York and working as a dance teacher, Frenchie met Minnie Schönberg, a harpist whose mother *also* played the harp, and whose dad was a (non-harp-playing) ventriloquist.[1]

The two married in 1885,[2] and Minnie soon started popping out comedy legends. Leonard was the opening act, soon followed by Adolph, Julius, Milton, and, a decade later, Herbert. These names aren't familiar, because the brothers attended a poker game in 1914 with comic Art Fisher.[3] An actual comic strip called "Knocko the Monk" had sparked a craze for nicknames ending in *o*, and so Fisher gave "chick"-obsessed Leonard the nickname Chicko (later shortened to Chico). The stern Julius became Groucho. And the third-generation harpist Adolph—who had presciently already changed his name to Arthur—was dubbed Harpo.

The boys didn't plan to go into comedy. Growing up poor on New York's Upper East Side, young Groucho wanted to study medicine. But the

1. Minnie's brother was another famous vaudevillian, Al Shean. In one routine that has somehow survived on *YouTube*, he said he didn't notice the *Venus de Milo* has broken arms ("Where were you looking, Mr. Shean?"). This stuff killed in the 1920s, dear reader.

2. They claimed they were married in 1884 so they could pass off Minnie's illegitimate niece Polly, born in January 1885, as their child. Groucho was named for Polly's stepfather, Julius.

3. As with most things Marx Brothers–related, the specifics of this story are disputed.

family needed money quickly, so he was pulled out of school at age twelve, making Minnie probably the first Jewish mother in history to tell her son *not* to become a doctor.

Groucho's brothers soon joined him in a singing group that had moderate success. They were once performing in Texas when someone ran into the theater to announce there was a loose mule outside. The singing must not have been great, because the audience ran out to see the mule. After everyone was reseated, Groucho started cracking wise—in such a situation, after all, the "ass" jokes practically write themselves. The crowd loved it, and the Marx Brothers switched to comedy.

After touring the country making people laugh, the boys decided to try out the silver screen. During the shooting of their first film, a screening was held in the Bronx. It went so poorly that production was stopped, and Groucho burned the negative. They went back to the stage and eventually had hit Broadway shows, inspiring two films—1929's *The Cocoanuts* and 1930's *Animal Crackers*—which both became huge successes.

The brothers would go on to star in many more classics, five of which made the American Film Institute's list of the 100 funniest movies of all time. Those gems include:

- **Duck Soup**, a political satire that was banned in Italy by the normally chill Duce of Fascism, Benito Mussolini.
- *A Night at the Opera*, which gave its name to a 1975 Queen album that fittingly enough found guitarist Brian May playing harp on one track. Queen's next album was named for another AFI entry, *A Day at the Races*.
- **Horse Feathers**, about a football game between Darwin and Huxley colleges, a reference that assuredly now goes over most viewers' heads (and we won't tell if you look it up real quick).

—M.S.

Q. The play *Everybody Comes to Rick's* was adapted into what classic film?

A. Casablanca.

During the summer of 1938, New York schoolteacher Murray Burnett and his wife traveled to Vienna, but they weren't there to send postcards and get new stickers for their steamer trunks. Three months earlier, the Nazis had swiftly annexed Austria, so Burnett was helping his Jewish relatives move their money and valuables out of the country.

After that emotionally charged not-a-vacation, Burnett went to the French Mediterranean, where he found himself in a nightclub surrounded by exiles, expats, and refugees from all over Europe. He sketched out some story ideas and, along with cowriter Joan Alison, turned a French gin joint into Rick's Cafe Americain, the centerpiece of a play they hoped would be a Broadway hit.

It wasn't.

They couldn't find a producer for *Everybody Comes to Rick's*, but in January 1942, Warner Bros. bought the play for an eye-popping $20,000.[1] The studio kept the bar as the setting for their eventual film, which they simply called *Casablanca*.[2]

It all worked out: In 1998, the American Film Institute called *Casablanca* the second-best movie ever (behind the seriously not-as-good *Citizen Kane*). When it was released later in 1942, Casablanca was all over the news—not because of Ingrid Bergman's fictional freedom fighting,

---

1. About $300,000 in today's dollars. This was unheard-of for two first-time nobodies; for *The Maltese Falcon*, Warner Bros. only paid well-known noir dude Dashiell Hammett $8,000.

2. The play finally debuted in 1991, in London. It closed after a month.

but because of the actual World War II. The movie premiered in Hollywood ahead of schedule, to coincide with the Allies' capture of the real-life Moroccan city of Casablanca.[3] The Warners even got some unofficial PR from Franklin D. Roosevelt and Winston Churchill, tying its wide release to a summit they were holding there.

Mind you, not a single scene was actually *filmed* in Morocco. Rick's Cafe Americain only existed on the Warner Bros. studio lot, and the dramatic final scenes were shot at the Van Nuys Airport. Regardless, the film inspired countless travelers to visit Morocco…and also inspired several other movies, including:

- ***Carrotblanca.*** An animated short starring Bugs Bunny as Rick, Penelope Pussycat as Ilsa, and Pepé Le Pew as her problematic admirer. I am shocked—shocked!—to find that feline harassment is going on here.
- ***Barb Wire.*** Roger Ebert pointed out that Pamela Anderson's 1996 dumpster fire has the exact same plot as *Casablanca*, only bad. Here's, um, not looking at you.
- ***Out Cold.*** A 2001 screwball comedy that boasts an 8 percent rating on *Rotten Tomatoes*. Among the downhill montages and *American Pie*–style gross-out jokes, you'll see the guy from *Dazed and Confused* put the gal from TV's *Wonderfalls* on a plane with actual Olympic snowboarder Todd Richards. Out of all the ski lodges on all the mountains in all of Alaska…

Unbelievably, there wasn't a real Rick's Cafe in Casablanca until 2004, when former American diplomat Kathy Kriger had the good sense to open one. Its beaded lamps, roulette wheel, and in-house piano player provide

---

3. "*Casablanca* will take the [box offices] of America just as swiftly and certainly as [the Allied Forces] took North Africa," *Variety* gushed in December 1942, because *Variety* has never had chill.

perfect reminders of that black-and-white time when everyone could agree Nazis were the bad guys.

Doubly unbelievably, Murray Burnett never went to the Moroccan city. "I never had any desire," he once said. "Maybe I don't want to destroy the image of Casablanca which I created."

Oh well. We'll always have Paris.

—J.C.

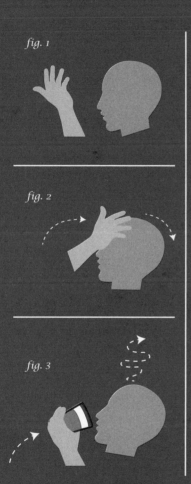

fig. 1

fig. 2

fig. 3

2

JOCK

SCRAPS

Q. A bird named Poe is the mascot for what NFL team?

A. Baltimore Ravens.

Once upon a Monday evening, Cleveland's team was gasping, heaving,
Somehow having gotten down around the Steelers' twenty-four.
I, upon my old recliner, felt my heart was in a grinder—
Never mind their good position; they were never going to score.
"Throw the effing ball," I begged and pleaded, hoping for that score.
Thirteen-three, a major bore.

'Twas the week after announcement of the owner's grim pronouncement,
Which left town and franchise shaken to their mediocre core.
Dogs for birds and brown for violet, Art Modell said to the pilot:
"Take this chartered plane and steer it to the Mid-Atlantic shore!"
Said the pilot, "Please be more specific—where upon the shore?"
Quoth the traitor, "Baltimore!"

Four years later Art was grinning, as his Ravens kept on winning,
Even Super Bowling, trolling Giants fans with thirty-four.
Lewis won MVP laurels—there's no prize for keenest morals—
All of it just made Ohio hate Art Modell even more.
What did he care? Twelve years later, they'd be champions once more.[1]
Off in stupid Baltimore.

1. This was Super Bowl XLVII in 2013, the one where John Harbaugh's Ravens beat brother Jim Harbaugh's 49ers 34–31, in a game that was spiced up by a brief power outage in the New Orleans Superdome. Beyoncé did "Crazy in Love," Budweiser ran that heartwarming father/son Clydesdale ad—and in fact, Art Modell didn't enjoy *any* of it, because he died the previous September.

So yeah, the Cleveland Browns moved to Baltimore in 1996,[2] taking their Ravens moniker (and mascot) from that "nevermore" poem by ghoulish homeboy Edgar Allan Poe. More on him:

- Despite his strong association with Baltimore, he and his *original* hometown of Boston regarded each other with bemusement and disdain. But time heals all wounds: in 2009 Boston dedicated an Edgar Allan Poe Square, and in 2014 they added a suitably creepy statue of the man and his imaginary black bird.
- "The Raven" wasn't the only Poe-m that mentioned a woman named Lenore. She was the title character in another poem in which the narrator pines for her because, you know, she's dead. Mind you, if you took out all the dead pretty ladies with unusual names, Poe wouldn't have much of a portfolio at all; just ask Annabel Lee, Berenice, Eleonora, Eulalie, Madame L'Espanaye, Ligeia, Madeline, Morella, or Ulalume.
- Staying on-brand until the end, Poe's 1849 death—he was found delirious and in strange clothes on a local election day, and died days later—is a famously unsolved mystery. The most interesting theory[3] is that he was a victim of "cooping," a form of voter fraud where men keep hostages huddled in a tiny room (a coop, if you will). Then they liquor 'em up, give them opioids, change their clothes repeatedly, and strong-arm them into voting at multiple polling stations. For the love of God, no one tell Fox News about this theory.

—J.T.

2. Officially, the Ravens became a *new* franchise, which just happened to keep the entire infrastructure of the team that mysteriously disappeared from Cleveland that same season. The current Browns began play in 1999 and inherited the sad, sad history of the old team, which they've honored by posting a losing record in eighteen of their first twenty seasons.

3. Except maybe the rabies theory. Rabies is always interesting.

Q. The Phoenix Suns' mascot, Go, is what kind of animal?

A. Gorilla.

No, gorillas are not native to Arizona.

The Suns had no mascot before one night in 1980,[1] when the Eastern Onion singing telegram service[2] dispatched a fur suit–clad twenty-three-year-old named Henry Rojas to Veterans Memorial Coliseum. As Rojas was leaving, he did a little tap dance under the home basket to a Herb Alpert song. A referee tossed him a ball, and Rojas sank the foul shot. The crowd went crazy, and a legendary mascot was born.

Rojas's gorilla specialized in a kind of slapstick vaudeville, mocking opposing teams with props and well-scripted routines. He especially loved it when the Portland Trail Blazers came to town because he got to wear obnoxious plaid trousers in imitation of coach Jack Ramsay.[3] His routine that's often cited as the most outrageous was against the Knicks. During a time-out he emerged in a fedora to Frank Sinatra's "New York, New York," with several pieces of garbage stuck to his legs. Halfway through the song, a

---

1. They had once flirted with the idea of (seriously) an anthropomorphic sunflower. Do keep that image in mind as you read the rest of this essay.

2. Still operating, and still offering gorilla-grams—though nowadays its nearest office to Phoenix is some 600 miles away in Reno, Nevada. It is, of course, a terribly hilarious parody of Western Union, which stopped its own singing messenger service in 1974. Apparently, it's hard to let "Go."

3. When Ramsay died in 2014, *The New York Times* ran a typical file photo: red sport coat, blue shirt unbuttoned to the mid-chest, and what could easily be mistaken for rented bowling shoes. His basketball was better than his sartorial skills—in 1977, Ramsay led the Blazers to their first—and still only—NBA championship.

group of muggers charged him and beat him up. He staggered away as the crowd roared—take *that*, um, urban blight.

Rojas retired in 1988, handing over the gorilla costume to gymnast and acrobat Bob Woolf, who beat out five hundred auditionees by performing a flip dunk on a trampoline. Now semi-officially named "Go," the new gorilla would emerge from a tunnel through a wall of smoke and fire, waving a Suns flag, accompanied by cartwheeling cheerleaders. At halftime he performed monstrous trampoline dunks, landing on soft gym mats—at a 2001 playoff game, he even jumped through a flaming hoop.

Woolf is still around and also operates a Phoenix trampoline park, but in middle age he's increasingly been aided by a youthful dunk team called the Sol Patrol. In 2005, Go became part of the inaugural class in the Mascot Hall of Fame. He has since been joined by such luminaries as:

- **Jazz Bear**, the Utah Jazz NBA mascot, whose portrayer was fired in October 2018 for "undisclosed reasons." Being Utah, that could just mean he was seen drinking coffee in public.
- **Mr. Met**, the beloved New York baseball mascot who flipped the bird at a fan in 2017. Honestly, you have to do *something* for fun at a Mets game.
- **Nittany Lion.** In 2009 the guy who played him was fired for underage drinking. "Thank God it's something minor," Penn State probably said.

Burnishing his own Hall credentials, Go's borderline bullying has at least once brought about positive change. In 1999, during a visit by zaftig former-Sun-turned-Sacramento King Oliver Miller, he wore a fat suit and danced to Jimmy Buffett's "Cheeseburger in Paradise." Miller threatened to sue, but later said the Gorilla had motivated him to lose weight. Ask your doctor!

—N.P.

Q. The Sons of Ben support the Major League Soccer franchise in what city?

A. Philadelphia.

If you paid attention for, like, 10 minutes in middle school history, you know that Benjamin Franklin invented everything from woodstoves and lightning rods, to swimming fins and an early version of the catheters your weird uncle orders from Fox News. But the one thing he couldn't piece together in his workshop was a functional relationship with his eldest son—at least not after the Revolutionary War.

William Franklin once had a close relationship with his dad, but they became permanently estranged over politics. William was a British Loyalist; Ben, obviously a full-on American Patriot,[1] was not having it. It's all complicated, but in 1782, shortly after the British surrendered at Yorktown, William left New York for London. He never returned to the United States—and Ben even effectively cut him out of his will, thanks to "the part he acted against me in the late war, which is of public notoriety."

Mind for the ages? Sure! Father of the year? Not so much.

A couple of centuries later, as of this writing, over two thousand Philadelphia men and women claim to be the Sons of Ben—and it has nothing to do with Franklin's epididymis.

In 2007, some eleven years after the MLS began play, Philadelphia—America's fourth-biggest media market—still didn't have a team. So, three local guys decided to take matters into their own, uh, six hands. They

---

1. Probably also the name of one of those Fox News catheters.

founded the Sons of Ben supporters' group[2] on January 17, Franklin's 301st birthday, campaigning hard to bring a club to their city.

No less an authority than then-governor Ed Rendell has credited the Sons with what happened just a few months later, which you can hopefully guess by now: the MLS relented, and the Philadelphia Union played their first-ever match in 2010.[3]

Mind you, the Union were just the city's first *MLS* club, not its first grown-up soccer club overall. Predecessors include:

- The **Phillies**, founded in 1894—eleven years after those *other* Phillies—as part of the American League of Professional Football, America's first. They, and it, lasted one season.
- The **German Americans**, who in 1936 became the first amateur side to win the US Open Cup. Five years later, for obvious reasons, they became just the "Philadelphia Americans."
- The **Philadelphia Fury**, whose 1978 founding investors included Peter Frampton, Paul Simon, and Yes keyboardist Rick Wakeman. They never had a winning season, but brothers and sisters, they *jammed.*

But back to the present: both the Sons of Ben and their beloved club are unapologetically…um, all about the Benjamin. The Sons' Jolly Roger–style logo has a skull immediately recognizable as Franklin's, thanks to the bifocals and unfortunately wispy hair. Their email newsletter is called the *'Nack*, a reference to Ben's own eighteenth-century moneymaker, *Poor Richard's Almanack.* And the Union's badge features a snake that's deliberately reminiscent of Franklin's famous *JOIN, or DIE* cartoon.

2. Not to be confused with the *other* Sons of Ben, followers of Jacobean-era playwright Ben Jonson—who wrote some decent-enough period pieces but definitely didn't understand the offside rule.

3. It was a 2–0 loss to another expansion team, the Seattle Sounders FC. So far as we know, Rendell didn't blame the Sons of Ben for the defeat.

The official motto of the SoBs is *Ad finem fidelis*, Latin for "Faithful to the end"—apparently *not* a Franklin quote, but still, if you listen just right, you can hear William spinning in his unmarked British grave.

—J.C.

Q. The 1933 World's Fair exhibition *Kay Curtis Modern Mermaids* evolved into what Olympic sport?

A. Synchronized swimming.

At the turn of the twentieth century, Americans were drowning, and not metaphorically. According to a federal report in 1900, drowning caused twelve of every 100,000 deaths—the highest accidental cause on the list, some 25 percent higher than railroad accidents. But breathe easy, dear reader; this story has a happy ending.

Since its origin as a solo endeavor, many names were tied to the artistic maneuvers we now call synchronized swimming, from "water ballet" to, for some reason, "scientific swimming."[1] Whatever the name, it was in Europe where the activity really began to take hold in the late 1800s. Music halls installed tanks and threw swimmers in 'em to entertain the beer-soaked masses.

The US got its first taste in 1908, as Australian "underwater ballerina" Annette Kellerman performed on the vaudeville circuit, eventually making a successful jump to Hollywood.[2] Organizations like the YMCA and American Red Cross took note, and they set about using musical swimming pageants to promote health and safety. By 1920 the drowning rate fell by more than half.

In the meantime, stunt swimmer and instructor Kay Curtis—whose hometown Wisconsin newspaper once called her "a youthful Annette Kellerman"—was making her way to Chicago. Commissioned by the

1. Trying it in the Thames during a 1724 visit to England, Benjamin "I Did Everything" Franklin used the name "ornamental swimming."

2. Called "the perfectly formed woman," she also roused America's dander (and/or libido) by introducing the leg-baring, one-piece bathing suit. Apparently, one was her magic number, though—in an interview shortly before her 1975 death, an eighty-eight-year-old Kellerman called the bikini "shameful."

World's Fair to promote the underwater lighting installed in their Lake Michigan lagoon, she rounded up sixty bathing beauties, the "Modern Mermaids," to do intricate choreographed routines, three times a day, for more than ten thousand enraptured souls each show. Mind you, swimming wasn't the only thing lighting up the 1933 World's Fair:

- In the shadow of a 200-foot thermometer was an exhibit called ***Living Babies in Incubators***. Fairgoers paid a quarter to watch premature babies from Chicagoland hospitals get lifesaving care from a team of doctors and nurses. You thought "operating theater" was just a figure of speech?
- Not to be outdone, two sideshow hucksters promised a ***Live Two-Headed Baby*** on the fair's midway.[3] The infant died on the eve of the fair, though, so they substituted a fetus in formaldehyde and accordingly changed the marquee from "Live" to "Real."
- Fine, here's a happy one: the ***Gorilla Villa*** offered glimpses of great apes doing household chores, such as sweeping and dusting. One of them, Massa, would go on to become the oldest living gorilla in captivity (at that time), dying at age fifty-four.

Back to the water: Esther Williams started *her* movie career in 1942, taking synchronized swimming to new heights of popularity. In 1952 she even played Annette Kellerman, in the biopic *Million Dollar Mermaid*.

Though it didn't reach official Olympic status until 1984—four years after Kay Curtis died—synchronized swimming was first *demonstrated* at the 1952 games. By then, the accidental-drowning rate was down to a measly 3.2.

—B.C.

---

3. The midway was actually invented at the 1893 World's Columbian Exposition, also in Chicago, where it was dominated by the world's first Ferris wheel. Neither of these midways is the reason why Chicago has a major *airport* called Midway, though—that's named for the tide-turning aerial battle in the Pacific theater of World War II.

Q. Pro wrestler "Stone Cold" Steve Austin fought his way out of the womb in what state?

A. Texas.

Born in 1964 as Steven Anderson—and, yes, within Austin city limits[1] — he had already changed his name once, to his adoptive dad's Williams. It's unclear whether the jump to Austin was a tribute to his hometown or to *The Six Million Dollar Man*.[2] Either way, he got the moniker in the late eighties from a guy named "Dirty" Dutch Mantel.

Mantel also pitched "Stevie Rage." Williams made the right choice.

But even with a surname in place, Austin didn't escape the litany of identity changes that is the usual lot of the professional wrestler. In World Championship Wrestling he was "Stunning" Steve Austin; in the World Wrestling Federation (later World Wrestling Entertainment) he debuted in 1996 as "The Ringmaster"…you know, because he was master of the ring. Soon after *that*, he pitched a ruthless heel character based on a mafioso called "The Iceman." That name was taken, but—perhaps inspired by a coke-fueled viewing of *Batman & Robin*—WWF writers gamely suggested such terrible names as Fang McFrost and Chilly McFreeze.

Enter Jeanie "Lady Blossom" Clarke, Austin's legit-English then-wife, who had played his also-English manager/valet in the WWF universe. In the

---

1. Thank goodness he isn't from the north Austin suburb of Pflugerville. Nobody wants to watch a guy named Steve Pflugerville suplex anybody, no matter how stone cold he may be.

2. A TV show in which former astronaut Steve Austin (Lee Majors), after being severely injured in an experimental jet crash, is rebuilt with fancy bionic parts and sent to work as a federal secret agent. If you needed this footnote to explain that, congratulations on being young!

midst of this demoralizing namestorm, one day she told Austin to stop sulking and drink his tea before it got "stone cold," thus coining one of history's best-known wrestling names in the most endearingly genteel way possible.

That sorted, there was just one last bit of branding to do. After beating Jake "the Snake" Roberts at King of the Ring in June '96, Austin took aim at his born-again Christian persona, co-opting the most famous reference in John's gospel by quoting "Austin 3:16" (his much-more-succinct version simply read, "I just whipped your ass"). That irreverent new catchphrase became one of the WWE's all-time bestselling T-shirts, and helped seal his induction into the WWE Hall of Fame—itself, perhaps predictably, the source of some more oddities:

- Even with 204 total inductees as of this writing, there's no actual physical hall of fame. If there were, it would likely be at WWE headquarters in Stamford, Connecticut—home of the American Crossword Puzzle Tournament, *Maury*, and *The Jerry Springer Show*, and not far from the PEZ Visitor Center in Orange.
- Unkillable legend Ric Flair has been inducted twice, once as a member of 1980s and 1990s collective The Four Horsemen. The supremely confident Flair has called himself many things over the decades, but "the Jimmy Page of pro wrestling" isn't one of them.[3]
- Pete Rose was inducted in 2004, because the heavily scripted WWE has very little reason to care about gambling.

Other Hall of Famers include Joan Lunden, Snoop Dogg, and Donald J. Trump—and, yes, even Jake "The Snake" Roberts, whether or not Stone Cold said so.

—J.H.G.

---

[3]. Guitar player for both The Yardbirds and Led Zeppelin, Page is double-entered in the Rock and Roll Hall of Fame.

Q. To mix a John Daly, you add vodka to what non-alcoholic drink?

A. Arnold Palmer.

The universally loved winner of sixty-two PGA Tour events, Arnold Palmer seemed to luck into quite a few of his major branding opportunities:

- His fan base, Arnie's Army, came about after a bunch of GIs happened to get free Masters tickets in 1959, and ended up in his gallery. Palmer claimed not to even know who originally coined the phrase.
- While arguing with some business associates about a logo for Arnold Palmer Enterprises, Arnie once got irritated and walked outside. It happened to be raining, and he saw a woman open a multicolored umbrella. It's appeared on all his merchandise since then.
- One day, his wife, Winnie, was fixing up some iced tea. "Hey, babe, I've got an idea," Arnie said. "Make a big pitcher, and we'll just put a little lemonade in it and see how that works."

As for that last story, of course, it worked especially well. Palmer drank this unnamed concoction for years on the golf course—but it wasn't until he ordered one at a country club in Palm Springs, California, that a woman overheard him, and then asked her waitress for an Arnold Palmer. Boom: name established, legend made, and AriZona Beverage Company partnership (eventually) secured.

Being nonetheless a humble man, Palmer said he felt weird ordering the drink; instead of an Arnold Palmer, he would just ask for an iced tea with about a third of lemonade in it.[1]

If Palmer was a warm, fuzzy cardigan sweater of a human being, then John Daly is a walking mullet haircut: lots of fun, not too responsible. After winning his first PGA Championship out of nowhere in 1991, Daly got the nickname "Long John" for his prodigious driving distance on the course. He also became known for his drinking, smoking, colorful pants, distinctive hair, less-than-athletic build, and legal troubles—by early 1993 he had entered rehab for the first time, and been arrested for assault. Did you think *Happy Gilmore* was purely fictional?

Anyway, at some point in there, somebody added a bit of Russia's finest to an Arnold Palmer, and the "John Daly" became a fairly solid country-club joke. Daly caught wind of this and, always up for a quick buck, started selling his own prepared version of the beverage in 2012, under the also-solid brand name "Grip It & Sip It."[2] Apart from his canned cocktail, Daly is sponsored by Loudmouth (where one gets those psychedelic trousers), Rock Bottom Golf, and John Daly Pizza. In his free time, he makes country rock music, collaborating with the likes of Darius Rucker, Willie Nelson, and Kid Rock.[3]

Unlike Happy Gilmore, he has never beaten up Bob Barker—but then again, we're not sure he's ever *met* Bob Barker.

—L.T.

1. The official AriZona version uses a fifty-fifty ratio. We're guessing no one ever "corrected" Palmer on his own recipe.

2. After being picked up by cops outside a Hooters restaurant, Daly himself put the booze down for good in 2008. What we're saying here is, sober or no, it's hard to picture the man *sipping* anything.

3. At the 2018 Bass Pro Shops Legends of Golf celebrity shoot-out, Kid Rock sank a 40-foot putt, earning props from Jack Nicklaus, and finished in second place. The winner? Larry the Cable Guy.

Q. Margaret Court was a world number one in what sport?

A. Tennis.

She is, in fact, the tennis player with the most major titles of anyone, man or woman—twenty-four by herself, and another forty in same-sex and mixed doubles[1]—in the sport's history.

Born in 1942, not far from Melbourne,[2] Court was seventeen when she won the 1960 Australian Championships (later called the Australian Open) on her second try. For good measure, she took the next six too; through to the end of her heyday in 1973, she had won eleven of the thirteen Australian titles she tried for.

With arms 3 inches longer than the average woman's, and a conditioning regimen practically unheard of among female athletes of her day, Court dominated matches on other continents as well. Says the International Tennis Hall of Fame, "Some of her accomplishments need a second read to make sure they're not a typographical error." Over her career she won 92 percent of her singles matches and a record 192 singles tournaments. In 1970 she became the second of three women ever to complete a calendar-year Grand Slam.

Eye-popping though her stats were, she was just one of a long golden generation of Down Under tennis legends:

- **Roy Emerson**, a fellow career-slammer whose Australian dominance overlapped the first half of Court's: he won all but one of the tournaments held between 1961 and 1967.

1. You'll see what we did there.

2. But closer to Wagga Wagga, closer still to Wangaratta, and within veritable spitting distance of Wodonga.

- **Evonne Goolagong**, who missed out on a career slam thanks to the US Open, where she was runner-up for four straight years. But she's perhaps best known for her world-class rags-to-riches story: Raised in a legit dirt-floored tin shack, a member of the only Aboriginal family in town, at a time when the government was snatching such children for white-centric re-education, she learned to play with an unstrung racquet made from a fruit crate. She caught on quick, taking her first major title at nineteen.
- **Rod Laver**, the only player of either sex to win *two* calendar-year slams, in 1962 and 1969—i.e., on either side of the open-era line.[3] He's on anyone's greatest-ever short list, and the Australian Open's center court bears his name.

The complex's third-biggest court is named for…uh, Court. But that honor is increasingly under fire: the former Catholic converted to Pentecostalism, and in the 1990s, got ordained as a minister. Now, in between normal, constructive Christian stuff like feeding the homeless, she's a very, very outspoken critic of Australia's 2017 law allowing same-sex marriage.

And so, an epilogue: having won eighty-nine of ninety-two *women's* matches going in, Court got demolished in a 1973 exhibition match against fifty-five-year-old (and male) Bobby Riggs. Four months later her (female) rival Billie Jean King thrashed Riggs in the famous "Battle of the Sexes," viewed by ninety million people worldwide. Today, King concerns herself with many social justice causes. After years of defending Margaret Court, when asked at a 2018 press conference about her court, King said, "If I were playing today, I would not play on it."

King came out as gay in 1981.

—C.D.S.

---

3. Court's detractors will remind you that she played half of her career before the dawn of the "open era," i.e., before professionals were allowed to play in the major tournaments. The same rule kept Laver out for five years in the absolute prime of his career. But in Court's defense, the 1969–73 seasons were all post-open era, and she won eleven of the twenty majors during that span.

Q. The annual Rose Bowl Game is played in what stadium?

A. Rose Bowl Stadium.

Legendary college football announcer Keith Jackson wasn't talking about the stadium when he coined the phrase "The Granddaddy of Them All." The game came first!

Pasadena's Valley Hunt Club organized its first New Year's celebration in 1890, promoting "the Mediterranean of the West" and its bounty of winter flowers. From the beginning, the Tournament of Roses Parade was the marquee event, beating out even *Ben-Hur*-inspired chariot races.[1]

The event outgrew the club by 1902, and the tournament organization opted to add some football. But the first game didn't go quite as planned— some eight thousand people showed up, eight times as many as the organizers expected, to watch Michigan put Stanford's eggheads in their place with a 49–0 drubbing. For a while after that, the Tournament of Roses tried to lure folks in with stunts like a race between an elephant and a camel. It wasn't until 1916 that they remembered people would rather see football.

Sure enough, the crowds came back. In 1920 the city of Pasadena bought a literal dump in the Arroyo Seco area as a site for a new stadium. The tournament raised construction money by selling seat subscriptions. Total cost: $272,198.26, or about enough to hire L.A. Chargers third-string cornerback Jeff Richards for the 2018 NFL season.

The stadium and game both officially became the Rose Bowl on New Year's Day, 1923. The stadium is now a US National Historic Landmark, partly

---

1. The massively bestselling book, by former Union general Lew Wallace, was ten years old by that point. Charlton Heston was negative thirty-three.

because it is the reason why every postseason college game is called a "bowl," whether it makes sense or not.[2] The Rose Bowl is venerated for its heavenly grass, a location that wantonly uses the golf course next door as a parking lot, and a history of some of the best college football moments ever seen:

- In 1948, the first televised game, Michigan matched that 1902 outlier by beating Southern California 49–0. Fritz Crisler, coach of the fifteen-point favorite Wolverines, had warned them before the game about overconfidence.
- In 1988, Southern California erased a deficit to Michigan State and had the ball deep in Spartans territory with a chance to win. Instead, USC quarterback Rodney Peete fumbled at the Spartan twenty-nine, and they lost 20–17.
- In the 2006 title game, Texas upset two-time defending champions Southern California. USC squandered a twelve-point lead in the fourth quarter, inexplicably benching Heisman-winning tailback Reggie Bush at a crucial clinching moment. Heisman runner-up Vince Young ran in for the final, dynasty-killing touchdown. *(Ed. note: the writer is a UCLA alumna.)*

Mind you, gridiron is not the only kind of football that has made indelible marks on the nation's sports psyche at the Rose Bowl. At the 1999 FIFA Women's World Cup Final, on top of a dramatic home-team championship secured on a penalty shoot-out in front of ninety thousand screaming fans, we also got the legend of Brandi Chastain's bra.[3]

Keith Jackson's granddaddy could not be reached for comment.

—L.C.

2. Our historic favorites: The Poulan/Weed Eater Independence Bowl (1990–97), the Crucial .com Humanitarian Bowl (1999–2003), and the succinctly named Salad Bowl (1948–55).

3. Nowadays, shirtless celebrations earn an automatic yellow card—whether you're a man or woman, and whether you've got a bra under there or not. The NFL is not the only No-Fun League, you know.

Q. Soccer legend Petr Čech retired with zero career goals, having played what position?

A. Goalkeeper.

When Southampton FC visited Stoke City FC on November 2, 2013, the home side hadn't won since the end of August. It was hard to imagine anything but another week of *meh* in the West Midlands. But 13 seconds after kickoff, Potters defender Erik Pieters passed the ball back to goalkeeper Asmir Begović, who tried to boot it to the halfway line. Instead the ball was caught by the wind, took a couple of weird-ass bounces, and wound up in Southampton's net. There was nothing Saints keeper Artur Boruc could do but mutter Polish expletives to himself, as he rolled the ball back toward the center circle. That fluke of a goal—which was later equalized, for a meh-indeed 1–1 draw—was measured at 301 feet, 6 inches, and certified by *Guinness World Records* as the longest goal ever.

On the same day, Chelsea keeper Petr Čech uncharacteristically let two shots slip past him, as the Blues' six-game win streak was snapped by perennial mid-tablers Newcastle United. It was Čech's 302nd appearance between the sticks for Chelsea—and yet another match in which he didn't score a goal. By the time he retired in May 2019, Čech had appeared in 781 matches for his assorted professional clubs, and another 124 for the Czech Republic national team,[1] collecting more terrifying skull fractures (one) than goals (nil).[2]

1. He left the national team in 2016. Maybe if he'd stuck around another year or two, he could have knocked in a fluke goal against Liechtenstein or something.

2. He's easy to pick out in photos, thanks to the protective helmet he's worn since 2006. During a match against Reading that year, Čech took a hard knee to the noggin and wound up needing metal plates in there. He has said he has no memory of the three days that followed the game. *Sakra!*

That's not to say that Čech isn't accomplished: his four Premier League titles, four FA Cups, two European trophies, and four Premier League Golden Gloves are indisputable proof that he's Better Than You. And keeper goals are still a complete novelty in the Premier League; Begović's two-bouncer was just the fifth one ever.[3]

Some other notable goalkeepers have made it onto scoresheets:

- In 2016 **Oscarine Masuluke** scored a jaw-dropping stoppage-time bicycle kick for South Africa's Baroka FC. Because of that dazzler, he became the first goalkeeper to ever be nominated for FIFA's Puskás Award, given annually to the scorer of the world's "most beautiful" goal. He finished second, behind actual striker Olivier Giroud.
- Paraguay's **José Luis Chilavert** is the only player to score a hat trick during a game in which he was also the goalkeeper. On November 28, 1999, he banged in three penalty kicks for Vélez Sarsfield during a 6–1 win. He also took home the match ball, probably because nobody wanted to tell a guy nicknamed "*El Buldog*" that he couldn't have it.
- The 131 career goals by **Rogério Ceni** are the most ever by a keeper. A free-kick and penalty specialist like Chilavert, at one point he was the top scorer for Brazilian club São Paulo for two straight years.

In 2018, *FourFourTwo* magazine put Petr Čech at number two on its list of the best goalkeepers in Premier League history. It probably isn't worth noting—but only probably—that the top keeper on the list, Peter Schmeichel, *did* score once.

Just saying.

—J.C.

---

3. The other four are Peter Schmeichel; Paul Robinson; and two Americans, Brad Friedel and Tim Howard.

Q. Baseball surgery namesake Tommy John played what position?

A. Pitcher.

Tommy John was in the middle of a very good 1974 season for the Los Angeles Dodgers, just a few innings shy of qualifying for the National League's fifth-best earned run average. Instead of making that next clinching start, though, he heard what might have been the death knell for his career: he blew out the ulnar collateral ligament (UCL) in his pitching elbow.

Throwing a baseball with spin, at upward of 95 miles per hour, is perhaps the most unnatural movement in all of sports. Without that ligament to secure the elbow joint, it's just not possible to generate the forces necessary to pitch. In any case, John had little to lose by agreeing to undergo an experimental surgery, in which Dr. Frank Jobe would replace the damaged tendon with a healthy one from his non-throwing arm.

John spent the entire 1975 season rehabbing the elbow,[1] and the next year he became the first player ever to return to baseball after a UCL tear. In fact, he didn't just return—he flourished.[2] John scored three of his four All-Star Game selections after the surgery, and racked up more than half of his 288 career wins. His career stretched to a remarkable twenty-six-year

[1]. With help from Mike Marshall, a fellow pitcher, who had a PhD in kinesiology and helped John change his pitching motion to put less stress on his joints. We hope he got a bonus for that!

[2]. The experiment worked out for Jobe too—when he died in 2014, he garnered obits and memorials not only from the Dodgers and ESPN, but from *The New York Times* as well. If there were an All-Star Game for orthopedic surgeons, he'd have been a shoo-in for that too.

Geeks Who Drink Presents: Duh!

span, including two seasons as baseball's oldest active player. He retired in 1989, at the ripe old age of forty-six.[3]

In the first twenty years after 1974, a total of twelve players underwent what came to be known as Tommy John surgery. In the two decades after *that*, there were three hundred such procedures in the majors, spiking at thirty-six in 2012 alone. Three main factors are credited for the, erm, explosion:

- As early as high school, kids are specializing in baseball year-round rather than just in the spring. That leads to more innings pitched, less rest, and a higher injury rate. But at least it keeps them off our lawn!
- Average velocity is increasing. Throwing the ball harder means more force and more stress on the elbow. It also makes you, objectively, the coolest kid in school.
- The success rate of the surgery has improved, so players are more likely to opt for it rather than just rehab, preventative measures, or even retirement. If all your friends jumped off a bridge…

In 2018, thirty-three-year-old reliever Jonny Venters hurled his first big-league innings since 2012, becoming the first pitcher to return to the majors after a *third* Tommy John surgery. Lest you wonder, he doesn't have three non-pitching arms—doctors can also harvest un-blown UCLs from cadavers.

"It's *fronkensteen*," his surgeon may or may not have said.

—T.C.

---

3. He even played long enough to give up two hits to his dentist's kid in 1986. His dentist was John McGwire; the kid, Mark, went on to a successful—if medically enhanced—career of his own.

Q. The San Francisco 49ers officially joined the NFL in what year?

A. 1949.

The fact that the 49ers joined the NFL in a year ending in 49 had nothing to do with the California gold rush or its centennial. That just happened to be when the NFL merged with its short-lived competitor, the All-America Football Conference (AAFC), which brought in two teams that still play today (the other being the Cleveland Browns).[1] This was only the first of many things that coincidentally recalled the gold rush.

First, let's calibrate the machine. The 49ers' red-and-white uniforms had gray accents until 1964, when someone finally stopped overlooking the obvious and trimmed them with "Forty-Niner Gold." A totally conscious choice, this earns just one of a possible five Coincidence Nuggets.

Since 2014, the 49ers have been playing at Levi's Stadium in Santa Clara, California. Though Levi Strauss & Co. is popularly associated with the gold rush—it profited from the resulting economic boom, and catered to working-class folks who still panned the rivers—it wasn't founded until 1853, when the phenomenon was tapering off. And in any case, the only reason why the stadium is named for Levi's is that they straight-up paid for that.[2] The joint gets four Nuggets.

---

1. In its four seasons, the AAFC blazed a few trails. Owners put their teams on planes, while NFL teams continued to travel by rail; the league fielded twenty black players, before Jackie Robinson broke baseball's color line; and the Browns won all four AAFC championships. Unbelievable feats, all.

2. They paid $220 million for twenty seasons, beating out thirty-one competing bids. The team never said who all the losers were, but we'd totally go see a game at The Dropbox.

Geeks Who Drink Presents: Duh!

The 1849 gold rush started after James W. Marshall found gold in a river on John Sutter's property in Coloma, California. Sutter was just a prodigious landowner, and Marshall just a dude he hired to build a sawmill; neither seemed an especially great target for destiny. *But*, about 140 years later, a linebacker coach named John Marshall helped the 49ers win two Super Bowls in nine years. John Marshall, coaching for a team built on the legacy of guys named John and Marshall? A full five out of five Coincidence Nuggets.

But that's not all! Here are some even more tenuous connections we came up with:

- The 49th parallel north forms that long, straight portion of the border between Canada and the US. Originally designated in the Treaty of 1818, the border location was reinforced by James K. Polk's Oregon Treaty, signed in 1846[3]—one hundred years before the 49ers' first AAFC season.
- Indium's atomic number is 49. Named for the bright indigo color it makes when burned, the ductile metal was first isolated by German chemist Hieronymous Theodor Richter in 1864—exactly a century before the 49ers got their gold stripes.
- Hallie Quinn Brown was born during the 1849 gold rush, and died around the time of the 1949 AAFC merger. The first woman to earn an MS from historically black Wilberforce University, she taught with Booker T. Washington at the Tuskegee Institute, and worked on Calvin Coolidge's reelection campaign. Coolidge became president the *first* time when Warren G. Harding died—*in San Francisco*. Did you just get goose bumps?

—L.M.P.

3. Before that, the US and UK both claimed twelve degrees' worth of land in the Pacific Northwest, between what is now the Oregon-California state line and the tip of the Alaskan panhandle. Nirvana could have been Canadian, and/or Bryan Adams could have been American. Good looking out, James K. Polk!

3

EAT ME!

Q. According to legend, a Chinese mandarin once gave British Prime Minister Charles Grey what gift?

A. Tea.

After Sandwich, Grey is probably the second-best-known English earl in America—and pretty much all Yanks know about either one is what he reputedly liked to put into his biscuit-hole.

Born in 1764, the second Earl Grey—the first being his dad, Charles Sr.—was a lifelong liberal Whig politician, elected to parliament at age twenty-two. He spent the next thirty years becoming a party leader,[1] ultimately getting elevated to prime minister in 1830. In less than four years at Downing Street, he got some important shit done: making things fractionally better for still-prevalent child workers, and fulfilling a longtime goal with the passage of the Slavery Abolition Act.

Of course, all that got overshadowed by the tea, which we're not even really sure he himself popularized. One common origin story suggests that the earl's wife, Mary Elizabeth, dug a gift of tea infused with bergamot oil[2]—dug it so much, in fact, that it became her go-to beverage for entertaining, and it soon was the talk of the lifted-pinky classes.

---

1. Apart from an interlude wherein he got frisky with the very-married Georgiana Cavendish, Duchess of Devonshire. His parents adopted their illegitimate daughter, and though the story traveled fast through London society, it didn't do much lasting harm to either party. It *did* inspire the 2008 film *The Duchess*, in which the earl is played by Dominic Cooper. Watch it with someone else so you can go, "Hey, that's the tea guy!"—it doesn't come up in the movie.

2. Perhaps from some diplomat, goes one theory, who designed the mixture especially to offset the hard water at Grey's Howick Hall estate. The citrus fruit is too tartly acidic to eat fresh, but its oil can also be found in perfumes, soaps, marmalades, and cocktails. It had VIP status long before the earl got hold of it—the word *bergamot* ultimately comes from seventeenth-century Turkey, where it meant something like "governor's pear."

If that doesn't do it for you, some other oft-repeated tales:

- Like the prompt says, it was a gift from a Chinese mandarin. He put some bergamot in there because all the cool kids were experimenting with flavored teas at the time.
- Like the prompt says, it was a gift from a Chinese mandarin. He'd stowed the tea and the bergamot next to each other in the ship's hold, so the citrusy flavor was just a happy accident.
- All that's a bunch of crap; it was created by a completely unrelated mid-nineteenth-century tea merchant named William Grey. He used the earl's title purely for the marketing value.

Mind you, actual fact-finding won't help you sort any of this out. The *Oxford English Dictionary* blog crowdsourced some research a few years back, finding the earliest reference to "Earl Grey's blend" in 1884, nearly forty years after Charles's death. That said, the idea of using bergamot dates to at least 1824, smack in the middle of his legislative career. *That* said, the bergamot oil was originally used to enhance substandard tea leaves—hardly a practice likely to be championed by a nobleman. It's quite the roller coaster of…um, tea history.

Wherever it came from, it clearly has a long savory history—and an even longer future: if you believe Star Trek,[3] we'll still be drinking it, hot, until at least the twenty-fourth century. *Make it so!*

—L.M.P.

---

3. Who doesn't?

Q. Switzerland's dairy farmers call it Emmentaler. What do Americans call it?

A. Swiss cheese.

The Swiss would like you to know that they can make more than just Emmentaler, thank you very much. After all, these are people who speak Italian, French, *and* German.[1] "Swiss cheese," therefore, *could* refer to any of such varieties as:

- **Füürtüfel**, which proves that "fire devil" is even cooler when you translate it with three umlauts. It's not just a clever name, either: there are habanero, jalapeño, and black peppers in there.
- **Appenzeller.** Beyond the standard gaggle of microorganisms, the makers of this hard cheese wash it in a mixture of wine, yeast, herbs, and spices. Ask for that treatment at your local spa!
- **Scharfe Maxx**, which sounds like a beer made by a porn star, but in fact is a raw-milk cheese with a pink rind, is described by its purveyors as having a "beefy pungency" and "sweet funk." So, really it sounds like a beer made by a porn star who went to Burning Man and...contracted dysentery?

---

1. Also Romansh, officially. Spoken by maybe forty thousand people, mostly in the canton of Graubünden, it's basically what happened when Roman soldiers barged in speaking Vulgar Latin, and it had a baby with a local Alpine language called Rhaetian. We can't find a way to say "what a scandal" in Romansh—after all, hardly anyone speaks it—but according to one online phrasebook, *tualetta* means "bathroom," and that's all you really need to know in any language.

Anyway, none of those has the big holes you think of when you picture "Swiss cheese," so Americans are mostly stuck with Emmentaler (named, by the way, for a valley near the Swiss capital, Bern).

There are a couple of theories on how those holes get there, neither of which involves a tunneling cartoon mouse. For a long time, it was assumed that they're the shapes of carbon dioxide bubbles released by the microbes in the milk—bacteria farts, if you will. But in 2015, a Swiss lab declared that it's not the bacteria at all; those holes are created by hay particles that float around in the barn.[2] Which explanation is less appetizing, we cannot say.

Emmentaler or otherwise, the Swiss do love their cheese: on average, each one eats 49 pounds per year. That's about 12 pounds more a year than Americans eat, though it's unclear whether our figures count quasi-cheese things such as Velveeta and Kraft Singles.[3]

Lest you wonder, the world's biggest cheese eaters are *not* the French, who eat about 59.8 pounds of cheese per person each year, coming in behind Denmark (62), Iceland (61), and Finland (60). At the other end of the scale is China, where they average less than 4 *ounces*. Apparently, "sweet funk" isn't for everybody.

—S.D.Z.

2. Agroscope, the lab, showed you can control the number of holes by adding different amounts of hay dust to the milk. Furthermore, they argue that Emmentaler has fewer holes than it used to, because modern milking methods mean that a lot less dirt gets in. Food scientists, just in general, are notorious party animals.

3. Famously, they are "pasteurized prepared cheese products," not cheese *per se*. Velveeta, once held up by the American Medical Association as a builder of "firm flesh," is a blend of dairy by-products, with lots of preservatives to keep it shelf-stable. *Bon appétit!*

Q. The company that invented Tater Tots was located near the border between what two states?

A. Oregon and Idaho.

It was 1952, and brothers F. Nephi[1] and Golden Grigg had a problem. From their facility in Ontario, Oregon, smack-dab on the Idaho border, they'd had great success selling frozen corn, and they'd just pivoted to French fries. The slicing, blanching, and flash-freezing techniques pioneered a few years earlier by potato baron J.R. Simplot offered up bushels of cash from a postwar market horny for frozen foods.

But alas, potatoes aren't perfect cubes, and the plant was producing more waste than the Griggs could stomach. They first fed the tater scraps to family livestock, but that was unconscionably wasteful to the young Mormon go-getters. There was money to be made!

You've probably guessed that their solution was the Tater Tot.[2] Sure enough, the Griggs ground up their scraps, added seasoning, and invented machinery to extrude the mush into the cylindrical little potato turds we know and love. Tots were frozen, par-fried, and shipped, and the innovation

---

1. In the Book of Mormon, Nephi built the ship that carried Israelites to the Americas. The civilization he founded was called the Nephites, and they flourished in the New World… until they turned wicked and were destroyed by the rival tribe of his brother Laman, who were Native Americans somehow. Nephi also had a divine vision of three witnesses who would vouch for Joseph Smith, and then wrote that vision down on the very golden plates that Joseph Smith would find thousands of years later, requiring him to get three witnesses to vouch for him. Lucky turn!

2. The name is still trademarked by Ore-Ida, despite being popularly genericized. Some other non-obvious examples? Bubble Wrap (Sealed Air Corporation) and Broccolini (Mann Packing Company).

almost literally put the Griggs' Oregon Frozen Foods Company—later Ore-Ida—on the map. Nephi called them "the hero profit item," and he was right: he found a way to sell his garbage, and school-lunch and dive-bar menus would never be the same.

The humble tot might be the Griggs' enduring legacy, but it probably shouldn't be. Nephi, especially, was a delightful loon, one of those corn-pone mid-century business titans who's equal parts genius and nuts. Consider his 1985 memoir, *Breefs by Neef* (seriously). In 284 pages, he offers up anecdotes, short stories, tips on your golf game, ruminations on marriage and hair tonic, and, of course, sage business advice. "You'll never go broke by taking a profit," he crows.[3]

When he wrote his own chapter in the novel-sized Grigg family history, Nephi said he had written many books, including *The Tater-Tot: A Success Story*. We honestly can't tell if he's lying, kidding, or bragging when he lists his other titles:

- *Aw Shucks! It Really Warn't Nawthin'*
- *Life Is Golf Is Life*
- *Neef Lite: Guaranteed to Be 80 Percent Less Serious*

On his death in 1995, Nephi's *Deseret News* obituary noted his one life regret: "I've never hit a golf ball as far as I've wanted to." But Neef got his wish posthumously, kinda: Ore-Ida's food service division was snapped up in 1997 by New Brunswick–based McCain Foods, and, twenty years later, some McCain hash browns were recalled nationwide because they were contaminated with shards of golf balls.

Unlike the tater-trash that went into that famous first batch of tots, McCain insisted the balls were "inadvertently harvested."

—A.R.

---

3. Largely thanks to nepotism and mismanagement, Ore-Ida went broke and sold to Heinz in 1965. Nephi took a profit.

Q. A woman once sued a radio station when she went to claim a cash prize, but instead got what candy bar?

A. 100 Grand Bar.

No one remembers their *Myspace* days fondly, but in May 2005, twenty-two-year-old disc jockey Jason Hamman made a post he particularly came to regret. Known as DJ Slick to the listeners of Lexington, Kentucky, Hamman carefully selected two emoji, set his mood to "High," and typed about what he'd planned for that night's show: "Since only 7 of you will actually be tuned in tonight[1]…HOT 102 is showing our appreciation to our loyal listeners with a chance to win 100 GRAND!!!!"

Norreasha Gill, a twenty-eight-year-old mother of three, was the lucky tenth caller—or so she thought. Instead of collecting a comically oversized check and peacing out to buy a minivan for her family, she learned from the station manager that the entire contest had been a joke: what she'd actually won was a second-tier Nestlé candy bar.[2]

Failing to see the humor, Gill promptly hired an attorney, suing the radio station and its parent company for breach of contract. The freaked-out station manager eventually offered Gill $5,000. "I said I wanted $95,000 more," she told reporters.

1. It was the finale of the fourth season of *American Idol*, in which Carrie Underwood out-sang Bo Bice. Underwood has gone on to score seven Grammys and a Guinness World Record for the most number-one country hits by a female artist. Meanwhile, Bice once sang the national anthem at NASCAR's Feed the Children 300.

2. Nestlé released the crisped-rice chocolate concoction in 1964, calling it the $100,000 Bar, and its bright red wrapper promised "a fortune in flavor." That made more sense at the time—to keep up with inflation, it should now be called 820 Grand. We'd still rather have a Baby Ruth though.

Not only was Hamman's prank stupid, especially by pre–*YouTube* standards, but it wasn't even original. Opie and Anthony were the O.G. assholes behind this stunt, disappointing a Boston caller named Craig after weeks of buildup, seven years before DJ Slick tried it. But instead of hiding behind the station manager, the pair paid off the bit on-air, telling Craig it would be hard to buy that new truck with a candy bar. "You guys are a bunch of douchebags!" Craig yelled before hanging up.[3] Poor-quality recordings of the call went viral—well, viral for the dial-up AOL era—and the entire thing was later revealed to have been staged in the first place. Those rascals!

Three months after Norreasha Gill filed her very real lawsuit against WLTO, the case was settled out of court. By that time, Hamman was no longer working for the station. No one seems to know what happened to the candy bar.

In any case, it's clearly not the only misleadingly named Nestlé product:

- **Oh Henry!** was created by someone named George.
- **Butterfinger** contains neither butter nor fingers.
- There has never even once been a tollhouse that accepts **Toll House Cookies** as payment.

—J.C.

---

3. He wasn't wrong. O and A's rap sheet reads like a worst-greatest hits of shock jock gags: they were fired from that station for a mayoral sex scandal/death hoax, then fined by the FCC for a song called "I'm Horny for Little Girls." Their partnership finally ended after nearly twenty years in 2014, when SiriusXM fired Anthony Cumia for a racist *Twitter* rant. Did you fill your bingo card yet?

Q. What New World spice tastes like a combination of cinnamon, nutmeg, ginger, and clove?

A. Allspice.

Hailing from the Caribbean Sea, the evergreen allspice tree is about as New World as it gets. Christopher Columbus himself brought it back across the Atlantic after his second expedition, thinking the berries were peppercorns.[1] In classic Columbus fashion, he wound up getting his wrong name for the stuff into dictionaries forever: in some places it's still called "pimenta,"[2] from the Spanish word for black pepper. Naturally, it was the English who later coined the name "allspice," because "pumpkin spice" wasn't a thing yet.

A couple millennia before Columbus, some of South America's Arawak people settled in modern-day Jamaica. They brought over their methods of smoking and drying meats, which included barbecuing with the wood of the allspice tree (*Pimenta dioica*).[3] Later, in the seventeenth century, a group of slaves called the Maroons escaped into Jamaica's Blue Mountains

1. We like to imagine this blunder was first discovered after a fifteenth-century patron said "when" to his grinder-toting waiter at the Barcelona Olive Garden, and then proceeded to eat the strangest salad ever. (It's up to you, dear reader, if you'd like to search *Urban Dictionary* for "Barcelona Olive Garden.")

2. Not to be confused with "pimiento," that actual pepper (*Capsicum annuum*) that always gets shoved inside olives, despite starting out bigger than the hole. (But enough about the "Barcelona Olive Garden.")

3. The Arawak called this meat-roasting rig *barbakoa*, and that's where "barbecue" came from. Another kind of grill was called *mukem*, which got Frenchified into *boucan*, and eventually—because some hunters turned into pirates, not because pirates were big hibachi fans—gave us "buccaneer." None of this has anything to do with "buckaroo," which comes from the Spanish *vaquero*, or "cowboy." Anything else we can look up for you?

and cohabitated with the native people. They shared a common interest, you see: avoiding the Europeans.

Eventually, the Arawak and African cooking influences combined, the meat getting poked with holes and filled with a blend that almost always included allspice, then cooked and wrapped in leaves for preservation. To the eternal delight of worldly middle schoolers, this process came to be known as "jerking"—and it gave us not only the modern dish of Jamaican jerk chicken, but the entire concept of jerky as well.

But wait, there's more! Some other uses for allspice:

- During the Napoleonic Wars, Russians warmed their feet—and made them smell better—with boots full of allspice powder. "The key to decisive victory is keeping your toesies cozy," Sun Tzu famously never said.
- The essential oil of the allspice tree is reputedly among the almost-literal potpourri of ingredients in Old Spice deodorant. Procter & Gamble won't confirm it, though, because they hate fun.
- The Mayans used it to embalm their leaders. Perhaps they used too much: one of the enduring mysteries of Mayan archaeology has to do with the great K'inich Janaab' Pakal, whose sixty-eight-year reign in the seventh century, in what is now southern Mexico, is the longest ever known in the Americas. His tomb was found in 1952, with an ornately carved sarcophagus that fueled ancient-astronaut theories. Those are unmysterious and plainly untrue, of course— but we're still not sure why the bones inside seem to be those of a forty-year-old. *Bum-bum-BUMMM!*

Alternative-medicine types use allspice for toothaches, for muscle aches, or as a poultice for wounds. And if you're not into any of that, you can, you know, just use it to consolidate your spice rack.

—J.T.

Q. Each year, the Indian district of Darjeeling produces 10,000 tons of what crop?

A. Tea.

In 1829, two British officers were dispatched to resolve an Indian-Nepalese border dispute. They stayed in a tiny one hundred–person village in the Himalayan district of Darjeeling and found the mountain climate so salubrious, they decided to establish a health resort there. Colonial tourism!

The government leased them the land and appointed Dr. Archibald Campbell of the Indian Medical Service to oversee the building of a Darjeeling sanitorium. Thanks to the efforts of legendary "plant hunter" Robert Fortune,[1] Campbell came into a supply of Chinese tea plants (*Camellia sinensis*),[2] which thrived in the cool, wet mountain climate.

Then, as now, Britons were drinking so much tea they might as well set up an IV drip, so Campbell got to work. He set up a nursery, which quickly became a garden. By 1866, Darjeeling had thirty-nine plantations covering more than 1,000 acres and producing more than 50 tons of tea each year—and it only grew exponentially from there.

---

1. Cooler than he sounds. In the 1840s the Scottish-born Fortune learned Mandarin, shaved his head, and grew a ponytail to blend into the Chinese population. After surviving various encounters with pirates and "xenophobic mobs" (his words), he managed to obtain twenty thousand plants and seedlings for the East India Company, and shipped them to the Himalayas in custom-made terrarium suitcases. He later introduced more than 120 Asian plant species to the UK, and published several books about his travels. Eat your veggies, kids!

2. Specifically the *sinensis* variety, whereas most Indian tea comes from the larger *assamica* plant. Darjeeling tea owes its stature to the unique combination of its Chinese origins and the unique misty climate of the Lower Himalayas.

When England finally left India alone in 1947, control of the plantations reverted to Indian businesspeople. Now in the province of West Bengal, Darjeeling underwent a Communist revolution in the 1960s, leading to violent clashes between owners and unions—reducing tea production, in other words, but improving working conditions. These clashes continue to this day. In the 1980s the industry was further hampered by an armed Nepalese separatist movement.

Meanwhile, the tea business was flooded with "counterfeit" Darjeeling, much of it from Sri Lanka, which involved mixing a small amount of the real thing with tea of much lesser quality. After much drama, the Tea Board of India petitioned the World Trade Organization (WTO) for special protection;[3] nowadays, only tea grown in one of eighty-seven certain Darjeeling estates can bear the name. The kerfuffle wasn't for nothing—real-deal Darjeeling is considered one of the finest teas in the world. The best comes from the "First Flush," or spring harvest, and exhibits the following qualities:

- A light, golden color when brewed. Dark-colored Darjeeling will not be of the best quality—or, even worse, fake.
- An aroma redolent of grape or muscatel. If you don't know what muscatel smells like, what are you even doing?
- Delicate, small tips, known (seriously) as Super Fine Tippy Golden Flowery Orange Pekoe. If your tea just says "Orange Pekoe," that's the lowest quality of Darjeeling whole leaf, and you may as well switch to Kool-Aid.

—N.P.

---

3. WTO rules tend to be very arcane. For instance, Cheddar cheese is not protected, even though it originated in the village of Cheddar, England. Stilton *is* protected, even though it's not actually made in Stilton. Other protected products include Newcastle Brown Ale, Colombian coffee, Idaho potatoes, and Vidalia (Georgia) onions. You can still make an Alabama Slammer anywhere, though.

Q. Not found in nature, what colorfully named fish is just a bigger, uncanned version of a sardine?

A. Red herring.

What a twist! Etymologists generally agree this figure of speech stems from a late-Renaissance practice, wherein poachers threw off canine trackers by leaving smoked ("red") fish along their scent trail. From there, it was a quick jump to metaphor: a 1782 speech in parliament mentioned "the red-herring scent of American taxation before they found out there was no game on foot." We don't know what that means, but we bet it's snooty.

To logic-philosopher types, a red herring is an informal fallacy—a statement expressly intended to misdirect or distract from an argument. As with many fallacies, the real problem is that it's so damned effective: wrote Robert J. Gula in his rhetorical study *Nonsense*, red-herring followers "forget what they were initially talking about; in fact, they may never get back to their original topic." Come on, people, you're smarter than dogs!

Of course, we know the term best from its trope-tastic deployment in mystery stories, since the dawn of forever. Communism was a red herring in *Clue*,[1] as was Miss Havisham in *Great Expectations*. But we didn't see the absolute zenith of the red-herring game until 2000, when novelist Dan Brown created Harvard symbologist Robert Langdon—you know, the tweedy all-purpose know-it-all portrayed by Tom Hanks in three movies thus far. Let's consider some of Brown's, erm, greatest hits:

---

1. In other words, the 1985 comedy film, whose screenplay passed through legendary playwright Tom Stoppard and composer/writer Stephen Sondheim, before landing in the laps of John Landis, who passed on directing it, and Jonathan Lynn, who didn't. Lynn went on to direct *My Cousin Vinny* and a bunch of episodes of something called *Yes, Prime Minister*. We don't know what that is, but we bet it's snooty.

- In ***Angels and Demons***, Swiss Guard detective Captain Rocher is, like Langdon and his dark-haired smart lady sidekick *du jour*, hunting for the antimatter that's threatening to blow up the Vatican. Our heroes think he might belong to the villainous Illuminati, but then...nope! Seriously, the character winds up being so inessential that the film omitted him altogether.[2]
- In the 2017 book ***Origin***, ultra-conservative Bishop Valdespino seems to be behind the assassination of Langdon's billionaire scientist buddy, who threatened to bring down all the world's religions with, you know, his sheer brilliance. But then it turns out Valdespino has always been down-low gay platonic buddies with the also-gay, also-conservative, dying Spanish king. *¡Que lindo!*
- ***The Da Vinci Code***'s Aringarosa—yes, a bishop again, and the head of shadowy, retrograde Opus Dei—has a name that straight up is Italian for "red herring."[3] Now that's what I call symbology!

If you suspect there's something interesting about the herring that makes it a good ironic-device candidate—well, that's a red herring too. It's silvery (not red) and superabundant (and *super* exploited), and even its taxonomic name is as boring as it can possibly be: the genus *Clupea* is the Latin name for the closely related shad, and the species name *harengus* means—have you guessed?—"herring." The only thing that's maybe *mildly* interesting is its many names as a foodstuff. Canned as a juvenile, it's one of the many small fish called "sardine"; smoked and butterflied as an adult, it's a "kipper."

Or is it?

—A.R.

---

2. Appropriately enough, the film was shot under the fake working title *Obelisk*.

3. Well, "pink herring." Brown was probably shooting for *rossa*, the real Italian word for "red," but left one of the *S*'s in the security office at the Louvre or whatever.

Q. Glen Bell was the founder of what fast-food chain?

A. Taco Bell.

Glen Bell's crunchy taco recipe has been going strong since 1952, when he first introduced it at his chain of roadside hot-dog stands. He birthed Taco Bell in 1962, in Downey, California; sold the chain to PepsiCo in 1978; and died in 2010. By the time he went to the big Enchirito in the sky, his namesake company had moved beyond selling different combinations of the same tiny list of ingredients, to mostly just selling straight-up gimmicks:

- To celebrate their fiftieth birthday in 2012, they partnered with corporate sibling Frito-Lay to create **Doritos Locos Tacos**, which, as the name suggests, have shells made with Doritos.
- In 2014 they convinced people to eat **Waffle Tacos**, a syrup-drenched fold of meat and eggs.
- Three years later, they gave us the **Naked Breakfast Taco** and a rip-off of KFC's Double Down called the **Naked Chicken Chalupa**.[1]

This sort of menu gimmick garners free advertising: people talk about them on social media, stand-up comics make jokes about them,[2] and they

---

1. The shell is made of fried chicken, you see. As for the ripping-off, it's all good, because Taco Bell and KFC are both part of the same mushy garbage-food collective, the PepsiCo spinoff that is (inaccurately) called Yum! Brands.

2. Remember 2007, when Patton Oswalt called one KFC offering a "failure pile in a sadness bowl"? *They still sell those!*

sometimes even get covered by the Serious News. In marketing and PR circles, Taco Bell are past masters of "earned media."

They've also done enough traditional promotions to put a minor-league baseball team to shame. On April Fools' Day in 1996, they claimed they had bought the Liberty Bell. In 2001 they floated a massive vinyl target near Australia, promising free tacos if it got hit by Russia's falling Mir space station. In 2008 they prompted an actual lawsuit by 50 Cent, when they publicly asked him to promote their value menu by changing his name to 99 Cent.

Anyway, food quality be damned, all the hustle seems to be working: Taco Bell insists that each year it sells two billion tacos worldwide, and a billion burritos to boot. One place where it's *not* selling is in Mexico—though they have made at least two hilarious attempts to sell the country on their "authentic American food."[3] The respective stores, in Mexico City and Monterrey, stayed open for a grand total of five years.

As for that original 400-square-foot location in Downey? It stood for fifty-three years, operating as a Taco Bell for about twenty-four of them. It was home to other taquerias until 2014, at which point there was talk of tearing it down. Instead, the next year, Taco Bell moved the tiny boring edifice 35 miles across Los Angeles, to its corporate headquarters in Irvine, California. Earned media, meet heritage preservation!

—P.S.P.

---

3. This isn't the only example of America's "authentic foods" being so different from their foreign inspirations that they're unrecognized in their ostensible homeland. Even Italian pizza is changing to resemble its American counterpart. Yoga has been cited as another example of the "pizza effect." We can't have nice things.

Q. What's the Polish word for *sausage?*

That's right, if you go to Poland and ask for kielbasa, you're going to get asked, "What kind?"[1] Have one of these answers handy:

- **Kielbasa mysliwska**, literally "hunter sausage," but it's made of boring old pork. This non-perishable snack is ideal for a long hunting trip, hence the name. If it's a solo trip, you could also take along a Carson McCullers novel—she wasn't Polish, but she did write *The Heart Is a Lonely Hunter.*
- **Krupniok.** It's a Silesian blood sausage, with some barley thrown in. This is the gateway to Eastern Europe, after all; there's gonna be some of this stuff.
- **Parówki.** Basically, the Polish version of a hot dog. If you ask for *parówki cielęce*, it'll be made from veal; if *parówki wieprzowe*, then pork. Those are the only kinds we know of—but in case you're curious, *Google Translate* says *parówki dront* would be a dodo-dog.

Poles have been stuffing meat and spices in casings since at least the Middle Ages—but after World War II, the Polish government decided that, like everything else in a proper communist society, the making of sausage should not be an individualistic endeavor. In 1959 the government published an official guide to meat products, including forty-six categories of

---

1. You'll also be told that you're saying it wrong. It's actually written *kiełbasa*, and the slash through the *L* means that you pronounce it like a *w* in English. So, "keow-BAH-sah."

sausage, er, kielbasa. There was even a Department of Meat Industry, to make sure nobody was calling their sausage something they shouldn't be.

Poland shook off its communist regime in 1989 and joined the European Union in 2004, so now everyone's free to rock out with their *krupniok* out. Some kielbasaficionados insist this was *not* a good thing, since capitalist factories use additives that they never needed behind the Iron Curtain. But there are hipsters in Poland just like everywhere else, so artisanal sausage is making a comeback (hold the systematic oppression).

In the New World, kielbasa can *really* mean big business. Consider New York's famous Gramercy Tavern, where the kielbasa entree will set you back $36. It's made from Wagyu beef and pork fat, with lumps of melty raclette cheese in every slice.[2] Another New York chef, Edi Frauneder, once told the *Village Voice* that in his native Austria, cheese kielbasa is thought of as drunk food—but he still makes Gramercy a regular lunch spot, hangover or no.[3]

The burning question you may still have in your head: what exactly do Polish people call the smoked, garlicky, pork/beef stuff that Americans call kielbasa? Turns out this is one of life's unanswerable questions. When we found an American who dared to ask in an online discussion where he could find American-style kielbasa in Poland, the answers from Poles universally boiled down to "That's not even a thing!"

So, when in Warsaw, don't be a *dront*: do as the Varsovians do, and expand your *kielbasa* horizons.

—S.D.Z.

2. You will not be served the whole sausage, which weighs about 10 pounds, and presumably costs about as much as a Fiat 500. (By the way: about 90 percent of the world's Fiat 500s—all of them except the ones sold in North America—come from Poland, where Fiat has had a manufacturing presence off and on for nearly a century.)

3. "The closest thing to Vienna sausage heaven," he called it. Sorry, Hormel.

Q. In the US, what word is embossed on Swedish Fish candies?

A. Swedish.

Known as *pastellfiskar* in Sweden—yes, "pastel fish"—these sweet little swimmers are made by the Malmö-based candymaker Malaco. Strangely, they're pretty quiet on the history of the candy, and have never even confirmed what fruit flavor the original red fish flavor is supposed to be.[1] But we know that it was in the 1950s that Malaco wanted a product to break into the American market. They settled on the now-familiar fish shape and boldly announced its provenance by stamping "Swedish" right behind the gills. By 1970, Swedish Fish were a weird little fixture at movie theaters, swimming-pool concession stands, and anywhere else you'd find people who aren't wearing braces.

Not actually gummies, the fish belong to a candy group called "wine gums," first invented by London candymaker Charles Riley Maynard in 1909. No one really knows why he called them that—they aren't even shaped like wine bottles—but (a) Maynards Wine Gums are still going strong in the UK, and (b) according to legend, Charles's dad didn't want to eat them, because he abstained from boozing. Mind you, they're totally free of alcohol.

But back to Scandinavia: despite their chewy texture and piscine form, Swedish Fish can still be eaten by vegetarians; unlike gummies (and even the original wine gums), they contain no gelatin.

To indulge alongside other nationally appropriate things, try these:

---

1. Many have speculated it's lingonberry, a tart staple of the Scandinavian diet (and the grocery section at IKEA). The berries and leaves can also be made into medicine to treat urinary tract infections—but we don't recommend trying that with Swedish Fish.

- **ABBA** was Sweden's first musical act to be enshrined in the Rock and Roll Hall of Fame. Not only did they do "Take a Chance on Me" and "S.O.S.," but they also contain an actual princess: in 1992 Anni-Frid Lyngstad married Prince Heinrich Ruzzo Reuss of Plauen, whose family, from 1806 until World War I, ruled a tiny principality in what is now the German state of Thuringia. See that girl, watch that scene, et cetera.

- Play with **Dalecarlian horses**. These carved wooden horses, traditionally painted Swedish-fish red with a white and green saddle, began as a kids' toy in the 1620s. In the New World, giant Dala horses stand in several upper Midwest communities that were originally settled by Swedes—even though their descendants would rather play with iPads.

- Literally just Swedish for "death cleaning," ***döstädning*** is when aging people throw out most of their possessions. It's meant as a generous gesture toward the next generation, which is spared the drama of figuring out what to do with all that inherited stuff. The parents get less clutter for themselves[2] and a tangible starting point for grappling with end-of-life issues—rather than just emotionally gorging on Swedish Fish.

By the way, if you ever want to catch an actual Swedish fish, we'd recommend Lake Vänern. Found in the southwest of the country, it is nearly as big as the whole state of Delaware, and it's chockful of trout, salmon, pike, and something called zander. Once you catch them, go ahead and carve the word "Swedish" right into their sides—we won't tell![3]

—K.S.

2. Margareta Magnusson's *The Gentle Art of Swedish Death Cleaning* was published a few years after Marie Kondo's *The Life-Changing Magic of Tidying Up*. The 2010s have truly given us a mother lode of mucking out.

3. Seriously, though, don't do that. What is wrong with you?

Q. What was the name of the Benedictine monk who allegedly invented champagne?

You know the story: in 1693, Pierre Pérignon, the blind head of an abbey in Hautvillers, France, had been dicking around in the wine cellar with a new method. Upon sampling his delicious, sparkly creation, he called out, "Come quickly, I am tasting the stars!" From there it was all Gucci and Gulfstreams…if the story weren't a bunch of crap.

The so-called *méthode champenoise* takes juice from several grapes—generally Pinot Noir, Pinot Meunier, and Chardonnay—ferments them separately, and makes them into a sour blend, or *cuvée*. That cuvée is then bottled with sugar and more yeast, and secondary fermentation occurs in the bottle. When yeast eats sugar, it poops carbon dioxide, and, hooray, you get bubbles.[1]

But alas, Pérignon didn't invent any of that. The Dom just figured out that blending grapes from different vineyards produces a properly acidic cuvée that re-ferments just the right amount. He also helped develop a gentler press to get white juice from black grapes, which is better for re-fermentation.

If that all sounds underwhelming, that's because it kind of is. We know about Pérignon today just because his abbey successors pumped up his rep to move product—and because more than two centuries later, Moët & Chandon

---

1. This wouldn't have been possible without "English glass" bottles that don't explode when you re-ferment. The English *really* don't want you to forget this, nor that they're the first ones who liked sparkling wine. So next time you run into an English wine chauvinist, remind him that in 2018, exactly zero of the UK's ten top-selling wine brands were English-made.

named their prestige champagne after him. Pérignon's famous "quote" first appeared in nineteenth-century advertisements[2] and is 100 percent made-up.[3]

Pérignon is far from the only monastic type to contribute to the world of booze. Switzerland's Saint Gall monastery has the world's oldest known brewery plans, from around C.E. 820, and Trappist ales are still some of the world's most sought after. Whiskey was invented by Irish monks, Chartreuse by Carthusians, Benedictine by Benedictines (duh), and we owe the entire California wine industry to some tipsy Franciscans.

But monks have given us non-intoxicating things too:

- Cistercian monks in Yorkshire, England, invented the blast furnace in the 1300s. By figuring out how to recycle hot air through a furnace, they achieved much higher temperatures, removing impurities from molten iron to make it stronger. This sparked widespread medieval use of iron as a construction material…and eventually led to Motörhead. Thanks, Cistercian monks!
- The Augustinian friar Gregor Mendel planted a bunch of peas in the 1850s and 1860s, and thus gave the world the first sketch of how genetic inheritance works. The scientific world ignored his findings for a nice long time, because who cares about a monk's gardening project? But eventually Mendel's study provided the needed mechanism for change in Charles Darwin's roughly contemporary theory of evolution. Oops!
- In the sixth century the Buddhist monk Bodhidharma went from India to China, spreading the Chan philosophy (which later jumped to Japan and became Zen). According to legend, he also trained the men of Shaolin Monastery in kung fu, in order to defend against bandits. We've totally seen that movie!

—A.R.

2. Also the century that gave us ads for Joy's Asthma Cigarettes, Lloyd's Cocaine Toothache Drops, and various soap brands too racist to mention here.

3. While we're at it, his practice of blind-tasting grapes from different vineyards led to the story that he was blind. He probably wasn't.

Q. According to legend, what beverage suffered a sharp decline in US popularity around the end of 1773?

A. Tea.

There are "ragtag groups of fighters," and then there are ragtag groups of fighters. On the morning of August 6, 1777, two of the latter met in a wooded ravine alongside tiny Oriskany Creek in Central New York. Tipped off by Molly Brant, the Mohawk widow of Britain's superintendent of Indian affairs, British Loyalists knew a local militia was on its way,[1] with some Oneida allies, to help the Americans hold nearby Fort Stanwix. So now, Mohawk and Seneca—like the Oneida, part of the rapidly fraying Iroquois Confederacy—were hiding shoulder to shoulder with poor, white local Tories, all of them supporting the redcoats' effort to claim the Hudson River and sever the Continentals' northern supply lines.

It would be a rare Revolutionary battle fought almost solely among American volunteers; indeed, most had no fighting experience at all. But they got it fast: the ensuing ambush left over four hundred dead, and started a civil war among the Six Nations of the Iroquois.

From there, Molly's brother, the self-made leader Joseph Brant, became probably the best-known of all the Mohawks. Already a friend to Britain after the French and Indian War, he spent the early days of the American Revolution trying to drum up Iroquois support for the crown. He had conferred with both sides—in fact, in his life he personally met both Georges, Washington and The Third—and decided that only the king's men could

---

1. Previously wary of entering the conflict, the militia was emboldened by tall tales of a young white woman who had been recently killed and scalped by unspecified Native Americans. Sadly, 'twas ever thus: indiscriminate, racially fueled attacks typified both sides' actions throughout the Saratoga Campaign.

offer anything of value to his people, who had depended on trade with white settlers for some time. The Battle of Oriskany began his mostly undeserved reputation as the "Monster Brant":

- He was wrongly implicated in the Wyoming Massacre of July 1778, despite having been nowhere near there. The action itself, in which a reported 227 scalps were taken, was considered retribution for the few Iroquois losses at Oriskany—even though these were entirely *different* white patriots.[2]
- He was rightly placed at the Cherry Valley Massacre in November 1778, but his actions there were complex and disputed. He reportedly tried (mostly in vain) to minimize civilian casualties, but doubled back afterward to burn down a general's house and take an additional prisoner.
- Over just a few days in July 1779, his raiders burned down Peenpack, New York, then routed some would-be avengers, despite being outnumbered, at the Battle of Minisink. That's another name for the Delaware River, mind you; no kitchenettes were involved.

Eventually commissioned as a regular British captain, Brant would finish the war in defense of Fort Detroit. But his side lost, of course, and so he lived out his postwar days in Ontario, where he established its first Protestant church, called for unity among all tribes, and continued to try (again, mostly in vain) to secure land, protection, and rights for the reunited Iroquois.

Brant's connection to the essay prompt is tenuous but ironic: in December 1773, you'll recall, it was Mohawk garb that the Boston patriots wore while chucking tea crates off of three British ships at Griffin's Wharf.[3] Apparently, the Mohawks were not sufficiently flattered by this.

—C.D.S.

2. See what we mean?

3. Even though there were two separate Ebenezers involved, we hereby declare that the best participant name was Nathaniel Frothingham Jr.

Q. What was the name of the actual ranch operated by the inventor of ranch dressing?

A. Hidden Valley.

We humans have been stuffing our faces with greens for as long as we've been around—and writing about it for about as long as we've been writing:

- Aristotle extolled the virtues of red chard, and Virgil described a primitive Italian salad.[1] He didn't use that word, but, like *salsa* and *salami* and *salary*, it does ultimately come from the Latin for "salt."
- In Shakespeare's *Antony and Cleopatra*, ol' Cleo described her time with baby daddy Caesar[2] as her "salad days"—because she was so green, you see—giving us the perfect idiom for wasted youth.
- In 1937, American English got the phrase "salad bar." It wasn't a famous writer who coined it or anything; we just really like salad bars.

Anyway, it was during the English Restoration that one John Evelyn raised the veggie-journalist bar. A meticulous diarist on a myriad of subjects—theology, painting, and horticulture, to name a few—in 1699 Evelyn published *Acetaria: A Discourse of Sallets*, widely believed to be

---

1. Another phrase used in that Virgil work? *E pluribus unum*, or "from many, one," referring to the mixing of *moretum*, a pesto-like spread. It makes a weird amount of sense that American money has a snack recipe on it.

2. Julius, that is—not Caesar Cardini, the Italian-American chef who created his own namesake salad in 1924.

the first written instructions for making salads.[3] He specifically called out "dressings" as giving salad a "grateful gust and vehicle."

Assuming that means it makes them yummy, we couldn't agree more!

The artery-busting wonderfood that is ranch dressing can be traced directly to 1950s Anchorage, Alaska. That's where Nebraska plumber Steve Henson created the creamy original buttermilk and herb recipe to get his contractor crews to eat their vegetables. It worked, and upon returning to the contiguous forty-eight a few years later, he started serving it at his 120-acre dude ranch outside Santa Barbara, California.

Riding and shooting and fishing are fun and all, but city slickers kept coming back to Hidden Valley specifically for that creamy, delicious plumber dressing (he didn't call it that). Henson soon started selling packets of herb mix, to take home and add to buttermilk and mayo. When he got tired of that, he started selling prepared bottles. In 1972, he sold the whole Hidden Valley Ranch brand to Clorox (yum!). And by 1983, they had created a chemically altered recipe with an unopened shelf life of about half a year (yum again!).

Nowadays, ranch is clearly the king of your grocery's salad-dressing aisle: thanks to its widespread use as a dip for everything from broccoli to wings to pizza, it has twice the market share of its closest US competitor. You can't thank Henson directly—he died in 2007—but the next time you pick up a bottle, pour some out for him.

Or, you know, squeeze it out, depending on what kind of bottle it is.

—B.C.

---

3. A few years earlier, in 1690, he edited a version of a satirical pamphlet by his late daughter Mary, which we include here only for its magnificent full-page title. The pamphlet was called *Mundus Muliebris: or, The Ladies Dressing-Room Unlock'd, and her Toilette Spread in Burlesque. Together with the Fop-Dictionary, Compiled for the Use of the Fair Sex. The second edition, To which is added a most rare and incomparable Receipt, to make Pig, or Puppidog-Water for the Face.*

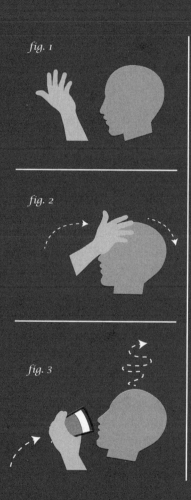

fig. 1

fig. 2

fig. 3

4

CORPORATE
FILTH

Q. In January 2011, *High Times* magazine put out a special edition to celebrate what issue number?

A. 420.

Put down the doobies, kids, it's time for some good old-fashioned magazine learnin'!

When *High Times* debuted in 1974, it was meant as a one-off *Playboy* parody with weed instead of boobs—even featuring a centerfold of some lucky dank plant that presumably wanted to rebel against its father. Surprising even themselves, they found a big market: by 1978, nearly four million people cracked an issue open every month, reading such helpful stories as "Dope Superlawyers," "Why Dope Gets You High," and "How to Fly Low."[1]

By the 1980s the magazine's focus became much more homegrown, with features such as "How to Grow 10-Pound Monster Plants." Unfortunately, the growing War on Drugs saw many of their advertisers raided by the Drug Enforcement Administration, desperately harshing everyone's mellow. In 2004, *High Times* even tried to leave its stoner past behind and become a serious literary magazine—but it only lasted a few months before a famous cover trumpeted, "The Buds Are Back."

In the era of widespread legalization movements, the buds are not just back—they're back with some serious economic motivations. In September 2018 the magazine began seeking pre-IPO investors—with investment perks kicking in at $420, natch. Average weed-smoking investors are in bizarre yet interesting company, among a number of B-list celebs and politicians—reggae scion Damian Marley put five on it, and former Mexican president Vicente Fox is on the board of directors.

---

1. Founder Tom Forçade's day job was smuggling, you see.

This baked-ass brain trust has put out some memorable covers since that lady in the panama hat considered a magic mushroom on the first cover in the dying days of the Nixon administration:

- In August 2015 they photoshopped former stoner **Barack Obama** with a star-spangled bong and a big thumbs-up, calling on the president to "LEGALIZE NOW." For some reason they did not use his campaign slogan, "Fired up, ready to go."
- In May 2003 *High Times* encouraged women to come out of the "cannabis closet," featuring the magazine's first named (and fully clothed) cover girl, "Hollyweed superstar" **Frances McDormand**.
- Way back in September 1977, gonzo journalist **Hunter S. Thompson** got the cover. He memorably told the magazine, "In order to get in the White House, I had to promise not to call anybody a Nazi cocksucker."

Though *High Times* didn't start obsessing over it until 1990, the number 420 entered weed-culture parlance three years *before* the magazine—and if you've ever insisted on sparking up at exactly 4:20 p.m., you'll be glad to know the phrase did indeed originate with the optimal time of day for indulging in that sweet, sweet ganja.[2] Specifically, it was a group of a dozen surprisingly responsible Northern California teenagers called the Waldos,[3] who once told a reporter, "The time we got out of school was approximately 3 p.m., but some of us had after-school sports activities that lasted until after 4 p.m."

I was gonna make a "higher education" joke here, but I forgot, *maaaan*.

—N.H.

2. Or date—after all, it was on April 20, 1898, that President McKinley signed a joint resolution to embark on the Spanish-American War. That doesn't have anything to do with pot, but, hee-hee, "joint resolution."

3. Because they hung out by a wall (seriously).

Q. The Diorama bag is made by what French fashion house?

A. Christian Dior.

Once upon a time, the task of carrying bags was reserved for servants and animals, and everyone else kept their small necessities tucked away in pockets. After World War I, however, carrying a purse became a symbol of independence for women, who increasingly had their own cash and cigarette cases to stash in those bags.

Christian Dior didn't found his namesake fashion house until December 1946, but when he did, he offered an escape to a France still recovering from the depredations of another World War. His first collection featured full-skirted dresses calling for an average of twenty yards of fabric, a prohibitive amount during wartime rationing. The exuberant collection was promptly christened the "New Look" by the press, a name it's been called ever since.

It was just a few years before Dior began licensing its name for handbags—as well as jewelry, furs, scarves, shoes, and ties. Introduced in 2015, a new Diorama bag[1] can set you back around $4,000, but it's hardly the only "it" bag Dior has put out over the years. There's also:

- The **Saddle Bag** (1999), shaped like the side of a horse's saddle (duh). It was snapped up by Beyoncé, Paris Hilton, and other

---

1. The actual dictionary word *diorama* was a French invention as well. Originally referring to a kind of translucent painting that showed two different scenes depending on the direction of the lighting, it was coinvented in 1822 by Louis Daguerre. One of his later creations, the daguerreotype process, was literally synonymous with "photography" from 1839 until about 1860.

real-life celebs, as well as *Sex and the City*'s Carrie Bradshaw. Discontinued after the early naughts, the bag made a comeback in Dior's fall/winter 2018 collection, and *Instagram* went *frénétique*.

- The **Lady Dior** (1994), with a more traditional shape—squarish, with round handles and some dangling charms to tell everyone "I dropped five grand on this bag," and a *cannage* leather pattern in imitation of Napoleon III–era chairs.[2] Officially nameless on release, the bag was later dedicated by Dior to a big fan: Diana, Princess of Wales.[3]
- **Diorever** (2016). Maybe it's too soon to tell whether this tote will become one of the greats—but Dior hired Jennifer Lawrence to shill it, so clearly they'd like it to be. *I volunteer!*

Christian died of a mysterious heart attack at age fifty-two, in 1957. His house waited until 1989 before they named a creative director who wasn't French—Italian Gianfranco Ferré—and it wasn't until 2016 that they picked a woman. Maria Grazia Chiuri's first Dior show channeled a book by Nigerian writer Chimamanda Ngozi Adichie, with T-shirts reading "We should all be feminists." Now *that's* our bag.

—S.D.Z.

2. The nephew of Napoleon I, and still the longest-serving French head of state since their revolution. He accomplished that feat with a self-coup: constitutionally barred from running for reelection after just two years in the presidency, in 1851 he dissolved the National Assembly, declared himself emperor, and set up a national referendum that showed the people were just fine with all that. In 1870 he personally surrendered at that World War prequel, the Franco-Prussian War. His exit marked the beginning of the French Third Republic, the one the Nazis took down.

3. Lady Di's first Lady Dior was a gift from Bernadette Chirac, then the First Lady of France. If she did it to promote French fashion, it was *très efficace*.

Q. In the McDonaldland ads, Captain Crook was singularly obsessed with stealing what sandwich?

A. Filet-O-Fish.

Ahoy, me mateys! Gather round for a tale as terrifying and tasty as has been told.

Started in 1971, the decades-long ad campaign featured various nefarious characters trying to get their paws on McDonald's products, only to be foiled by that crafty clown Ronald McDonald. The lineup of larcenists included:

- The **Hamburglar**, easily recognized by his Zorro-in-prison getup, "robble robble" catchphrase, and borderline-irrational love of beef.
- The **Fry Kids**. Originally called the Gobblins, the shaggy, ball-like creatures attempted to steal French fries—quite a feat, considering they have no arms. The "Gobblins" eventually became "Fry Guys" and then, when gender parity finally reached McDonaldland, got their third and final name in 1987.
- **Grimace**, an enormous purple monster first introduced as "Evil Grimace," who tried to steal milkshakes[1] with his two sets of arms. After horrifying kids for a year, in 1972 he lost the "evil" moniker

---

1. We're not sure why he has the only name in McDonaldland that isn't directly on the nose. Even so, "grimace" is totally what you do when you get milkshake-induced brain freeze—a.k.a. sphenopalatine ganglioneuralgia—which, lest you ever wondered, is just your cranky old brain reacting to the rapid temperature change in your mouth and telling you to knock it off. Yay neuroscience!

(and a pair of limbs), and joined Ronald's side in the righteous fight for…um, fast food.

And then, of course, there was Captain Crook. Inspired by *Peter Pan* in more than just his name, the red-coated and mustachioed pirate went after the Filet-O-Fish, a sandwich with a history all its own.

In 1962, Cincinnati franchisee Lou Groen decided he was tired of his heavily Catholic neighborhood ghosting on Fridays during Lent. He pitched a deep-fried halibut sandwich, but longtime CEO Ray Kroc wanted to try a meatless "Hula Burger" of pineapple and cheese on a bun. They set up a head-to-head challenge, and…well, even without hindsight, you can probably guess which thing people would rather eat. Grateful Catholics didn't even care when McD's immediately decided to save money by switching to cod (and later pollock); the Filet-O-Fish became the first non-burger sandwich on the nationwide menu, and to this day, 23 percent of them are sold during the forty-day holy season.

Back to McDonaldland: two years after the first wave of characters were introduced, *H.R. Pufnstuf* creators Sid and Marty Krofft successfully sued for copyright infringement,[2] forcing McDonald's to drop some of the characters—most significantly that burger-headed *Pufnstuf* look-alike, Mayor McCheese. Many of the original characters remained, though, and as the campaign plowed on, they added the breakfast-loving, hapless flier Birdie the Early Bird; the way-too-happy-to-be-eaten McNugget Buddies; and Ronald's dog, Sundae.[3]

---

2. The ad agency had even picked the Kroffts' brains for production tips, under the pretense that they would be getting the gig. Captain Crook isn't the only dastardly scallywag in this tale!

3. Dripping with jaded sarcasm of a very-nineties vintage, and played in live-action segments by Verne "Mini-Me" Troyer in a creepy costume, Sundae appeared in *The Wacky Adventures of Ronald McDonald*, a direct-to-video series produced around the turn of the millennium by *Rugrats* creators Klasky Csupo.

In 2003, McDonald's introduced the catchy "I'm Lovin' It" jingle, sung by all-ages favorite Justin Timberlake, and the quick-service Shangri-La came to an end after thirty-two years. The kids haven't seemed to mind—McDonald's never says for sure, but analysts estimate 15 percent of their US revenue comes from Happy Meals these days.

You know they're lovin' *that*.

—K.S.

Q. Olive oil and palm oil were the original main ingredients of what soap brand?

A. Palmolive.

In the summer of 1899, an unassuming advertisement started appearing in the Wisconsin paper, the *Oshkosh Daily Northwestern*. "Pharaoh's daughter and all other ancient royalty used for bathing just what is put in Palmolive," it read, "the proper thing for the Bath." Milwaukee's B.J. Johnson Soap Company[1] had been messing around with the formula of its bestselling product—the quintessentially Gilded-Age Galvanic Soap—by adding palm oil and olive oil,[2] two ingredients that are indeed associated with ancient civilizations.

To say it caught on like wildfire would not be exactly true. It took some fancy marketing—like a coupon for free Palmolive with every Galvanic purchase—to really make it stick with consumers. But by the 1910s they were putting beautiful and exotically illustrated full-color ads in all the ladies' magazines, still working that Cleopatra angle, and Palmolive was the world's bestselling soap brand. In fact, the company was so big that in 1928 it bought Colgate, a company that had been making toiletries since 1806 (including the first tubed toothpaste, in 1896), and even had its own namesake university (not a very big one, with about three thousand students today, but still).

1. Not to be confused with floor-wax magnate Samuel "S.C." Johnson—whose descendants still own that company after more than 130 years—or Johnson & Johnson, which, having been founded by brothers named Edward and James and Robert, should properly be called Johnson & Johnson & Johnson.

2. And cocoa butter, but PalmCocLive would be a pretty awkward name.

Today, Colgate-Palmolive makes everything from Hill's Pet Nutrition to Murphy Oil Soap, and they bring in $15 billion a year. But that doesn't mean every product has been a hit:

- Introduced in 1975, **Bambeanos** were roasted, flavored soybeans, meant to serve as a healthy snack around the time granola was getting popular. But there's a reason why beans are called "the musical fruit"; Bambeanos quickly got a farty reputation, and within a year they were pulled from shelves in a green cloud of ignominy.
- Brought to market in 1982, nearly four decades after frozen meals made their airline debut, **Colgate Kitchen Entrees** were not only late but truly bizarre. If you can imagine brushing your teeth with lasagna—on seeing the familiar red logo, customers clearly did—you'll see why this product line failed so hard that it purportedly even dragged down toothpaste sales.
- **Teen Spirit** deodorant has been on shelves for nearly thirty years, so it can't really be called a failure, but its main claim to fame was a pure misunderstanding. O.G. riot grrrl Kathleen Hanna[3] was in a grocery store about the time it came out and laughed at the bizarre branding. "What does teen spirit smell like?" she recalled thinking in an Australian radio interview many years later. "Like the smell when you throw up in your hair at a party?" Anyway, she was later hanging out with her friend Kurt Cobain, and wrote "Kurt smells like Teen Spirit" in Sharpie on his bedroom wall. Cobain, who presumably hadn't spent much time sniffing middle school armpits, thought the cryptic phrase would make a good song title, and Nirvana's "Smells Like Teen Spirit" became the definitive alt-rock hit of an entire decade.

—C.D.S.

---

3. Her two most famous bands are Bikini Kill, from the grunge era, and Le Tigre, from around the turn of the millennium. Their respective songs "Rebel Girl" and "Deceptacon" are required listening—as in seriously, go listen to them right now.

Q. SJP Collection is a shoe and handbag line created by what actress?

A. Sarah Jessica Parker.

If the shoe fits, Sarah Jessica Parker will wear it. And sell it.

As Carrie Bradshaw on HBO's *Sex and the City*, Parker boosted the shoes of Jimmy Choo, Christian Louboutin, and Manolo Blahnik. But afterward, in 2014, Parker partnered with Blahnik CEO George Malkemus III to start the SJP Collection, making handbags, little black dresses, and, yes, shoes—shoes with a trademark grosgrain ribbon centered on the back of the heel, covering the seam.[1]

Parker has said her priority was to make quality, lasting shoes that she would want to wear. In an interview in *The Daily Front Row*, Malkemus agreed: "Sarah Jessica wanted to do a collection for women who watched *Sex and the City* and were inspired by Carrie," he told the magazine. "But that character spent too much money on shoes;[2] she wanted her customer to be able to buy shoes that were affordable but beautifully made." Prices range from $250 to $600 per pair, so your mileage may vary.

Parker isn't the first—or last—celebrity Cinderella. Other famous folks who fashion footwear include:

1. The color of the ribbon changes each season. Parker wore similar ribbons in her hair as a child, which is also when she first found fame. After a bit of a hard-knock early life, she made her Broadway debut as an eleven-year-old in 1976, and even spent a year playing the title role in *Annie*. Leapin' lizards!

2. Indeed, in one episode, Bradshaw estimated her shoe collection at $40,000. "I will literally be the old woman who lived in her shoes," she quipped.

- **Daniel Day-Lewis.** The three-time Oscar winner left acting in 1997 to work for five years as a cobbler.[3] He returned to the big screen in 2017 for *Phantom Thread*, a movie about a twisted love affair between a high-end fashion designer and a woman schooled in the medicinal properties of wild mushrooms. We're not sure if this *entirely* counts as "write what you know."
- **Jessica Simpson.** The singer/actress/old-school reality star found her true fame and fortune through the Jessica Simpson Collection, a retail juggernaut in more than thirty product categories, most notably shoes. At one point, the business was somehow valued at more than $1 billion.
- **Ivanka Trump.** The first daughter's namesake shoe line was a victim of her father's presidency—Nordstrom, Hudson's Bay, and other retailers dropped it, citing poor sales amid a consumer boycott. The other shoe dropped in 2018, as Ivanka shut the line down altogether, officially citing her duties as a senior White House advisor. Mind you, by that time she'd had the job for eighteen months.

You can buy SJP at high-end department stores and in dedicated boutiques in New York, in Las Vegas, near DC, in Dubai, and in Abu Dhabi. Or anyway, you can try—in 2018, well-shod women waited more than 5 hours in line at the opening of the New York store to meet the SJP behind their SJPs. She still sometimes works the sales floor, as she told *The New York Times*: "I don't know how to be involved in another way."

That's what we call cash-and-Carrie!

—K.S.

---

3. Day-Lewis won the first of those Oscars playing Christy Brown, a man with cerebral palsy who was able to write, paint, and eat with his left foot, in the aptly titled 1989 film *My Left Foot*. But we checked, and Day-Lewis made his shoes for *both* feet.

Q. Archer Farms is a house brand sold by what retail giant?

A. Target.

When Minneapolis's Westminster Presbyterian burned down in 1895, the church raised replacement money by selling the next-door lot to parishioner George Dayton. A banker by trade, Dayton put up a six-story building, into which he lured a local dry-goods shop.[1] Within a year, he bought controlling interest in the store and named it for himself. Good ol' Midwest modesty!

The Dayton Company's next century-or-so featured boring stuff like mergers (J.L. Hudson), acquisitions (Marshall Field's and Mervyn's), and an IPO (1967). In '62, they opened their first discount department store called Target; by '75, the chain was Dayton-Hudson's biggest earner. The family's direct involvement ended in the eighties, after three generations, and the whole shebang was renamed Target Corporation at the turn of the millennium.

But Target's ascent to America's second-largest discount chain[2] also included actual innovations: the world's first store-owned radio station in '22, the US's first fully enclosed shopping mall in '56, and a 1920 delivery

1. Dayton's low-rise and the replacement church are both still standing. The former is a mixed-use retail/office space, with a Mary Tyler Moore statue out front (her namesake show shot its title sequence there). The latter is...a church. Smack between them, on Nicollet Avenue, you'll find modern-day Target headquarters.

2. The first-largest is the subject of *The United States of Wal-Mart*, a 2005 book by John Dicker. In 2006 Dicker cofounded Geeks Who Drink, the pub-quiz company whose book you're reading right now. As of this writing, Walmart is worth about $290 billion more than GWD.

from New York that they claim was the longest-ever commercial flight at the time.

Naturally, it hasn't all been airwaves and airplanes. Just consider two calamities from 2013. More than forty million credit cards were compromised in one of the world's biggest security breaches, and even the Secret Service got roped in to investigate. Details are still murky but—surprise!—Russians were involved.

They were also laid low in 2013 by a venture into Canada. Supply-chain problems boosted prices, compelling Canucks to find their ketchup chips and Fudgee-Os elsewhere, and ultimately resulted in a $2.1 billion blood-bath.[3] Not surprisingly, Target's chief information officer and CEO both "resigned" in 2014.

Since 1995, Target has launched several private-label brands: e.g., Market Pantry, Sutton & Dodge, and Simply Balanced. As for the O.G. Archer Farms, they once described their coffee as "farm-to-cup." An entire focus group, we imagine, went blind from their eyes rolling into the backs of their heads.

Now, for three cooler archers:

- **"Mad Jack" Churchill**, a British army officer (but no relation), known for arming himself with a long bow and a broadsword—*in World War II.* Yes, he killed at least one Nazi with a damn bow and arrow. As a commanding officer in Operation Archery (really), he once hopped off a landing craft as it descended upon the German garrison, playing a march on his bagpipes, before throwing a grenade and running into battle.
- **Jebe** from the Taichud tribe. Legend has him shooting Genghis Khan's neck with an arrow—non-fatally, to their mutual benefit. Instead of seeking retribution, Khan recruited Jebe to his side; he went on to be one of the Mongols' greatest generals.

---

3. By which we mean $2.1 billion US, not that loonie crap.

- **May Welland**, the symbol of innocence in Edith Wharton's *The Age of Innocence*. The book often compares her to Roman hunter goddess Diana, and eventually Wharton has her win a shooting contest before marrying the story's protagonist…Newland Archer. Seriously.

—B.C.

Q. The world's biggest jetliner, the A380, is a product of what company?

A. Airbus.

Airbus says, "Go big *and* go home!" At 239 feet long, with a 262-foot wing-span, the *Airbus A380* boasts a takeoff weight north of 550 tons, and can carry 555 passengers in…you know, what passes for comfort these days.

Why though?

As the new millennium dawned, Europe's Airbus and their US-based rival, Boeing, were both furiously rubbing their crystal balls, contemplating the future of aviation.[1] Eyeing the global air-travel boom, Airbus put together the world's biggest passenger plane,[2] aiming to lower fares by cramming each flight with the population of an average elementary school.

With a reported $25 billion development cost, though, the *A380* became something of a white elephant, the company having grossly overestimated how many travelers might enjoy longish LaGuardia layovers. See, thanks to its sheer physical size, the *A380* can only land at major airports with special facilities. Accordingly, Airbus has delivered just 230 of the things since its

---

1. Arguably, the *real* future of aviation had already come in 1967, when Boeing unveiled the *737*. More than ten thousand of the single-aisle jets have been built, and thousands more are still on order, making it the Toyota Camry of the skies (though, since the worldwide grounding of the *737 Max* in early 2019, Toyota might be less flattered by that characterization).

2. Meanwhile, Chicago-based Boeing proposed the *Sonic Cruiser*, an airliner that would travel just under the speed of sound. Neat! But the necessary fuel burn gave their accountants heart murmurs, so Boeing traded speed for fuel economy with the *787 Dreamliner*. Lame! They won this round of the fight, though; the *Dreamliner* has outsold the *A380* nearly three-to-one.

2007 debut—nearly half to Emirates Airlines—and announced in February 2019 that they'd stop making them altogether in 2021.[3]

The *A380* isn't alone in finding that more is sometimes less. Many of the other "biggest" planes were big flops too:

- The *Hughes H-4 Hercules* (length 219 feet/wingspan 320 feet), better known as the **Spruce Goose**, was billionaire Howard Hughes's answer to the bulk transport needs of World War II. Unfortunately, the wooden wonder didn't take wing until after the war ended, and was eventually relegated to an Oregon museum. Its geodesic hangar in California is now a cruise ship terminal. But hey, at least Cate Blanchett got an Oscar for *The Aviator*.

- The Soviets are not remembered for their whimsy, but the **Antonov An-225** (length 276 feet/wingspan 290 feet) looks something like a cross between Tinker Bell and Ivan Drago from *Rocky IV*. Built to carry rocket boosters for the Soviet space program, its 142-foot cargo hold is longer than the Wright brothers' entire first flight. Just one *An-225* was produced—but at least it's still flying! Since the demise of the USSR, it's been making charter flights with bits of power plants, wind-turbine blades, and whatever other enormous crap needs a-haulin'.

- Modern-day eccentric billionaire and Microsoft cofounder Paul Allen whipped out his checkbook in 2011 for the **Stratolaunch** (length 238 feet/wingspan 385 feet), featuring six Boeing 747 engines, twenty-eight wheels, and—why the hell not?—two fuselages. The idea is to strap a rocket between them, lift the whole thing up to 30,000-something feet, and then boost it right into orbit. Allen died in 2018, but you can't keep a good behemoth down; the *Stratolaunch* took its first test flight in April 2019.

—A.W.

3. The first specimen was taken out of service in 2017. As of this writing, it's being stored without its engines in a hangar near Toulouse, France. If you want it, you can probably get a nice pre-owned discount off the usual $440 million sticker price. Save your pennies!

Q. A guy saw his sister Mabel make mascara out of Vaseline and went on to found what company?

A. Maybelline.

The guy was Chicago-based chemist Thomas Lyle Williams. Corporate legend says Mabel was inspired to make her lash-darkening product after she singed her eyebrows and lashes in a kitchen accident.

Before then, mind you, women had been trying to figure out how to make their lashes longer and darker for millennia:

- A recipe in the Kama Sutra: make a powder from three different plants, apply it to the wick of an oil lamp, and put the resulting pigment on your lashes. Drugstores must have been much larger in those days.
- Roman historian Pliny the Elder mentions dyeing in his first-century *Natural History*. It's in his general description of the eyelashes, which he calls "an advanced bulwark against the approach of insects."[1] Eww!
- Ancient Egyptians made mascara from galena, a lead ore. We haven't checked with the surgeon general, but we're gonna go ahead and say that's probably not recommended anymore.

As for Williams, his original 1915 "Lash-Brow-Ine" formula was a colorless "enhancer"—at least until the founder of rival Lashbrow Laboratories

---

1. In the next sentence, he wrote that having too much sex could make your eyelashes fall out "not undeservedly." By Pliny's lifetime, lest you wonder, Aesop's "sour grapes" parable had already existed for more than six hundred years.

got his trademark struck down in 1921. By that point, Williams had developed a second product with some color in it, and slapped his sister's name on there.

More than one hundred years later, mascara still makes mad bank for the modern-day L'Oréal subsidiary. According to an oft-repeated factoid, a green-and-pink tube of Great Lash[2] is sold every 2.5 seconds somewhere in the world.

Part of that can be attributed to ad copy that's gotten steadily snappier since the original: "You can have beautiful, long and luxuriant eyebrows and lashes by applying 'Lash-Brow-Ine' nightly." The slogan *you're* thinking of, for instance, debuted in 1991—and a 2018 poll found that nearly 70 percent of respondents know "Maybe she's born with it. Maybe it's ____."[3]

One more recent campaign, ahem, laid it on a little thick. In 2013 an ad-industry group called out Maybelline for putting falsies on one of its models, resulting in lashes that are literally bigger than humanly possible. Perhaps to balance out its karma, in 2017 Maybelline got with the times and made *YouTube* makeup maven Manny Gutierrez its first male model. One homophobic columnist got salty, tweeting a photo of Gutierrez in Big Shot mascara and saying, "Dads, this is why you need to be there to raise your sons."

Gutierrez clapped back: "My dad actually works for me and is SO PROUD of me. Sorry bout it." Now *that's* some great lash.

—S.D.Z.

2. Those Palm Beach colors are no accident: the iconic tube was designed by resort wear queen Lilly Pulitzer, famous for her flamingo-and-fern prints in superbright colors. Sadly, they don't award a Pulitzer Prize for package design (but yes, Lilly married into that family).

3. This was good for a top-ten finish among the seventy-five slogans in the study. With a recall rate of nearly 88 percent, "finger lickin' good" came in at number one. If you're one of the other 12 percent…well, we'd rather not be the ones to ruin you.

Q. What company built the Italian Automobile Factory in Turin?

A. Fiat.

The year of our Lord 1945 was not an especially great one for Giovanni Agnelli:

- In March, Italian resistance agents informed him that friends of Benito Mussolini weren't allowed to run businesses any longer and that they would be taking interim control over Fiat—*Fabbrica Italiana Automobili Torino*, which he'd founded forty-six years earlier—for themselves, *grazie mille*.[1]
- In April, it became clearer that things wouldn't be going back to how they were, as the Resistance liberated Fascist North Italy. Mussolini himself, who had appointed Agnelli to the Italian senate in 1923, was found trying to escape to Franco's Spain, shot to death in a tiny town on Lake Como, then strung up outside a Milanese gas station for good measure.
- In December, Agnelli, uh, died. He was seventy-nine.

It was certainly a low point for Fiat—and indeed, all of Italy—but that only makes its/their resurgence all the more remarkable. The seeds of the comeback had been planted in the pre-war days: the original Fiat 500 came out in 1936, lighter than a cow at 1,200 pounds, and lumbering its way up to 53 mph thanks to an adorable 13-horsepower engine. In Europe, where they've always

---

1. It didn't much matter that Agnelli wasn't *really* a Mussolini supporter, just a businessman who would collaborate with anyone who could help him sell cars. What have we learned, children?

loved tiny cars, the "Topolino"[2] was a monstrous success. In two decades they sold half a million copies of that first design, and some car called the Fiat 500 has been sold somewhere in the world most of the years since then.[3]

Anyway, under newly promoted president Vittorio Valletta, Fiat became the best-known beneficiary of the Marshall Plan, parlaying $60 million in US and other funds (some $420 million today) into a rebuilt operation that made seven times as many cars in the 1950s as they had in the decade leading up to the war. In time they became Italy's largest privately held corporation, and acquired most of their Italian competition: Autobianchi, Lancia, Ferrari, Alfa Romeo, and Maserati. In 2014 they even bought one of America's Big Three, the Chrysler Group.

And much of this was under Giovanni Agnelli—a different one, the grandson of the original. He became president on Valletta's retirement in 1966 and set about doing standard things like bringing in new management and diversifying the product offerings. But mostly he was known as a fast-driving, jet-setting, ski-resorting, clothes-horsing captain of industry. Upon his death in 2003—fifty-eight years after Agnelli reenlisted in the Italian army, after their defeat, just to help drive the Germans out—then-Italian president Carlo Ciampi called him "one of the protagonists of the history of our country, expressing in every critical moment the fundamental values of the national character and identity."

Considering you can buy a Fiat at your nearest Dodge dealership. That may be an understatement.

—C.D.S.

2. It means "little mouse," and is also the Italian name for Mickey Mouse. In Chinese, he's *Mi Lao Shu*, which *Google Translate* helpfully suggests can alternately be read as "old rice mouse." But our favorite international name for Mickey is the Swedish *Musse Pigg*, *pigg* meaning "peppy."

3. The lightest ones are 2,366 pounds now. That other famous wee fascistmobile, the Volkswagen Beetle, has swollen from 1,760 to about 3,045 since 1938. If we make it past eighty, we probably won't be in the best shape of our lives either.

Q. Earl Silas Tupper is best known as the inventor of what product?

A. Tupperware.

When you look at the myriad bowls and mismatched lids in your pantry, you have one thing to be thankful for: industrial waste. Well, and DuPont. Hold your comments!

Around the time they were inventing useful things like nylon and neoprene, DuPont was also starting to bring in amateur R&D people, even letting them take home scraps from the plastics factory just to see what they came up with. That's how they found a failed tree surgeon named Earl Tupper, who stuffed his pressure cooker with some greasy, black, sludgy waste polyethylene.[1] He didn't get any superpowers, but he did get it to just the right consistency, dyed it an awful pastel color, *et voila!* Having already left DuPont to be an independent subcontractor, he got to name Tupperware after…um, his favorite home plastics chef.

But Tupper didn't make his millions right away. To take the brand global, it took the marketing genius of Brownie Wise (born Brownie Humphrey, before she decided her *surname* sounded silly). She liked the brand and started throwing parties to sell it to bored housewives; Tupper took notice and made her a vice president.[2] Wise recruited an army of suburban housewives to throw *other* Tupperware parties, and went on to create an

---

1. Other modern uses for polyethylene: toys, shampoo and detergent bottles, mop buckets, water pipes, plastic food wrap, cable sheathing, trash cans, gas cans, juice bottles, and those disposable grocery bags that are getting banned in all sorts of reasonable places.

2. Their partnership didn't end well. She was fired in '58, as Tupper found it hard to sell a company with a female executive. It worked: Rexall purchased Tupperware that same year. Sigh.

annual gathering called the Jubilee, where she gave away new cars, diamond necklaces, and dining room sets, just so everyone would know how easy it is to get rich in your spare time. The reality is different—we've checked, and the profit charts look eerily like a pyramid—but decades later, at least now you know which high school friends you need to block on social media.

At the top of the pyramid, drag queens have consistently ranked among the top ten of Tupperware sales reps in North America. Check it:

- Since 2004, actor Kris Andersson has been selling Tupperware as **Dixie Longate** (get it?), the star of a traveling stage show called *Dixie's Tupperware Party*, where you're legit handed a catalog and order form at the door, and encouraged to buy her "fantastic plastic crap." We'll take twenty!
- Self-proclaimed number-one seller from 2007 to 2010, Kevin Farrell is better known as **Dee W. Ieye** (get it?). His memoirs are called *Confessions of a Drag Queen Tupperware Lady*; says one *Amazon* reviewer, "I recommend the book and the muffin carrier."
- **Pam Teflon**, "the RuPaul of the Tupperware world" is perhaps the O.G. Tupperware drag queen;[3] she had a *Los Angeles Times* profile all the way back in 1996—in which she pointed out that her name contains *two* non-stick products. Again, we say, get it?

—B.C.

3. The latest Tupperware drag queen? Marge Simpson. In the 2018 episode "Werking Mom," she spiced up her sales by pretending to be a man dressed as a woman. Thankfully, guest star RuPaul was on hand to put it all in perspective.

Q. Dr. Klaus Märtens is best known for what occupation?

A. Shoemaking.

A medical doctor in the German Army during World War II,[1] Märtens sprained an ankle while on leave in the Bavarian Alps. He couldn't wear his standard-issue army boots, and so he made some comfortable-if-not-attractive alterations, in the true Teutonic tradition (hi, Birkenstock!), using soft leather and spent tires to create air-padded soles.

After the war, Märtens went on making boots with the same comfy, distinctive soles, using discarded rubber from the Luftwaffe airfields, and selling them with a college buddy named (seriously) Dr. Herbert Funck. German housewives embraced the shoes, with 80 percent of sales in the first ten years attributed to women over forty. Punk rawk!

By 1952, Märtens and Funck opened a Munich factory, and in 1960, British shoemakers Bill Griggs and family purchased the exclusive patent to make them in England. They fiddled with the heels, anglicized the name, trademarked the soles as "AirWair," and added the distinctive yellow stitching.[2] Mailmen, policemen, and factory workers all flocked to the boots with the soft soles. Meanwhile, a working-class subculture called "skinheads"

---

1. He's not even the Nazi you're most likely to find on your feet right now. Also during the war, adorably named brothers Rudolf and Adolf Dassler had a mysterious falling-out and split their shoemaking business into two separate companies called Puma and Adidas. This also means that, whatever you may dream about all day, Adidas is really just an eponym.

2. In Northamptonshire, about 65 miles north of London, where they're still headquartered today—though the Griggses cashed out in 2014.

had started up in the late fifties,[3] with a uniform of close-cropped hair, straight jeans, tight-fitting button-down shirts in check patterns…and DMs, as they called their boots. Soon enough, Docs had gained a cushiony foothold throughout Britain's youth culture.

Famous feet wearing Dr. Martens include:

- The Who's **Pete Townshend**, the first high-profile celebrity backer. He claimed the boots "released me from psychedelia and all the nonsense that went with it." Mind you, he started wearing them *before* he wrote "Baba O'Riley."
- **Elton John**, in *Tommy*. In 1975, The Who's rock opera was released as a film, featuring ol' Reg singing "Pinball Wizard" while wearing Docs lashed to four-and-a-half-foot stilts that also looked like Docs. In 1988, Elton sold the whole trippy rig to the R. Griggs Group.
- **Kurt Cobain.** The Nirvana front man paired Dr. Martens with busted jeans and flannel shirts, ensuring that for much of the 1990s, teen spirit looked roughly the same as it smelled.

At the height of the grunge wave, Dr. Martens opened a six-story boutique near the Royal Opera House in London's Covent Garden. Within a decade, though, the footwear fell flat and the company narrowly avoided bankruptcy.

Sales picked up again in the 2010s, as high fashion embraced the old working-class boot. Jimmy Choo, Vivienne Westwood, and Jean-Paul Gaultier collaborated with the brand, which also wound up on such decidedly *non*-downscale millennials as Gigi Hadid, Emma Watson, and Katy Perry.

They still look good with checked shirts and straight jeans though— maybe just take it easy on the buzz cut.

—K.S.

---

3. At first, they were apolitical, and in fact rallied around black rhythms from Jamaica to Motown. By the 1970s, though, some British skinheads got involved in racially motivated violence, and eventually the word itself took on connotations of white power and neo-Nazism. *That* was the part that got exported to North America. Lucky us!

Q. The Starbucks siren's crown is adorned with what symbol?

A. A star.

Starbucks iconography has taken on a sort of weird half-life in America—remember the furor over the all-red Christmas cup?[1] But all things Starbucks start with the famous two-tailed "Siren of Seattle" that adorns the company's cups, signs, aprons, and, one can only assume, Howard Schultz's thrice-damned soul.[2]

The original mermaid/siren was a bare-breasted rendition of a sixteenth-century Norse woodcut, according to the company, though others claim this origin tale is inventive corporate mythmaking. No matter: back in the simpler, halcyon days of Norse Woodcut Barbie, Starbucks was owned and operated by coffee-aficionado Seattle-ites Jerry Baldwin, Zev Siegl, and Gordon Bowker.

Schultz, the impresario who made it seem like a reasonable thing to have two branches of the same coffee shop literally across the street from each other, did not take the reins until 1987.[3] When he took the company

---

1. Do you wish you could forget? Like, a lot?

2. SuperSonics fans know what's what. In early 2019, as he was contemplating a bid to become president (of the US), Schultz devoted a page in his book, *From the Ground Up*, to a thirteen-year-belated apology for selling the beloved NBA franchise away from his adopted hometown and into Oklahoma Stupid Freaking City. *Apology not accepted, Howard!*

3. It's sort of startling to realize that the emergence of Starbucks as a globe-spanning, culture-crushing phenomenon is really, when you think about it, significantly more recent than the TV hit *Knight Rider* (which premiered in September 1982 on NBC). Much like the knowledge that Cleopatra lived closer to our time than she did to the construction of the pyramids, this temporal juxtaposition with the emergence of David Hasselhoff is…well, it makes us feel old, that's all.

public in 1992, the company had a meager 140 outlets and a stock valuation of $271 million; by 2018, those numbers were 28,000 and nearly $84 *billion*. That mermaid might as well have a dollar sign in her hair—they are making star*bucks*.

Which brings us back to that damned star. The O.G. Norse version of this watery tart *did* sport a crown, but it was star-less. The celestial adornment arrived with Schultz's corporate rebranding in 1987, as the corporate figurehead lost her nipples (but kept her belly button) and gained a five-pointed star atop her crown. Since then, the Starbucks siren has become one of the world's most recognizable logos, joining the illustrious ranks of corporate icondom, such as:

- Besides looking like "is ded" when you read it upside down, the tricolor **Pepsi** globe got its start as an image of a bottle cap in the 1940s. The current, more stylized version has a broad white stripe that's meant to resemble a smile. Go look in the fridge; we'll wait.
- In 1978 The Beatles' **Apple Corps** sued the startup Apple Computer over who gets to use a fruit so old that religious people think of it as the first fruit ever. After nearly three decades of back-and-forth, a final suit was settled when Apple Computer paid Apple Corps a reputed $500 million for full rights to distribute music under the name—and to stop bothering what would soon be the most valuable company in the world. Isn't it nice when an underdog gets a win?
- The **FedEx** logo has an arrow between the *E* and the *x*. It's in a book now, Internet; you can stop telling us this!

—A.W.

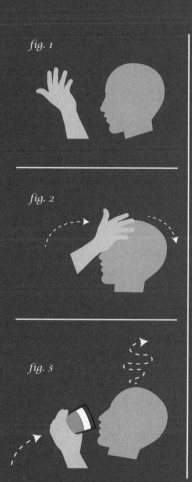

fig. 1

fig. 2

fig. 3

5

STATECRAP

Q. Who was the first US president without a law degree?

A. George Washington.

Not only did he not have a law degree, but Washington didn't go to college at all, or even secondary school.

Washington's two older brothers were much better educated, sent to private school in England by their dad, the moderately well-off planter Augustine Washington, who had been sent there by *his* snobby stepfather—after all, it was a great way to separate future generations from the other Virginia Colony hayseeds. Young George might have walked the same path, likely followed by a career in His Majesty's Navy, but instead ol' Gus up and died.

And so the eleven-year-old future president was bundled off to live with his half-brother Lawrence: a successful planter; pals with the influential Fairfax family; founder of the Ohio Company and the city of Alexandria, Virginia; and a militia veteran from the War of Jenkins's Ear.[1] Lawrence also owned a Potomac estate called Mount Vernon—or, as we know it now, "The Boring Monticello."

Anyway, George got a practical education under Lawrence's care, attending some day schools and hanging with itinerant tutors. He did get a surveyor's commission from Jefferson's alma mater, the College of William & Mary, but that seems to be about as close as he ever came to the hallowed

---

1. Apparently, a Spanish privateer cut off a guy's ear in (where else?) Florida, so naturally Britain had to invade South America. The sacking of Portobelo, Panama, inspired the first public performance of "Rule, Britannia!" that song from every movie that cuts to a London scene.

halls of academia. Then he learned law and economics through the daily grind of running a plantation.[2]

All of this probably made him into the dude America needed at the time. Instead of Chaucer in Cumbria, he surveyed the Ohio. Instead of ensign-ing on a Royal Navy frigate, he learned to resent the British, who turned him down for the regular army in the French and Indian War. In short, he was never able to think of himself as a Briton, just a Virginian, and a rube at that. Washington's lack of polish gave him a chip on his shoulder he took to the grave—and went a long way toward winning the American War of Independence.[3]

All told, twenty US presidents were never lawyers, degreed or otherwise, including:

- **Zachary Taylor** (years in office: 1849–50), who joined the army in response to something called the Chesapeake-Leopard Affair, and fought in all those other pre–Civil War wars you don't know much about. His sixteen-month White House stint ended abruptly when he died of...something. We're not saying he was poisoned by pro-Southern factions, but if we were, we would not be the first.
- **Teddy Roosevelt** (years in office: 1901–09), who dropped out of law school to write a book about naval tactics in the War of 1812, because of course he did.
- **Donald J. Trump**, which explains a lot. But not everything.

—A.R.

2. Or, you know, the daily grind of riding around and pointing at things while slaves did the actual work. At its height, Mount Vernon had over three hundred slaves. For his part, Washington manumitted the ones he owned outright upon his death in 1799, as did Martha in 1802. So that's...something?

3. In the aftermath of Yorktown, General Cornwallis pretended to be sick, and sent an underling to the surrender ceremony. Prickly-ass Washington refused to accept it and followed suit, directing Brigadier General Charles O'Hara to hand Cornwallis's sword to Major General Benjamin Lincoln. History has shown that, yes, it all still counted.

Q. The Parnas Lubricants company is based in what European nation?

A. Greece.

Indeed, if you need to lube up your chassis for the long road of etymology ahead, Parnas sells grease in drums up to 396 pounds!

That the country sounds like the friction-reducer is one of those (fairly frequent) English coincidences that means nothing. "Grease" comes to us from the Latin *crassus*, meaning "thick, fat, gross."[1] The name *Greece* is more of a mystery, but one thing seems pretty sure: if it weren't for a certain O.G. polymath, we'd probably call it Hellas (you know, like they do).

In his *Meteorologica*,[2] Aristotle briefly mentioned that the Hellenes used to be called Greeks. Had he realized he was about to change several languages for eternity, he might have elaborated a bit more. Anyway, a nineteenth-century theory places the word in an ancient town called Graea, literally "gray"[3]—and even then, "gray" also meant "old."

---

1. This, by the way, is not where we get our word *gross*. That comes from the Latin *grossus*, meaning "large" or "coarse." If you're one of those "English is too complicated" people, take heart: it's not all our fault!

2. It's exactly what it sounds like: an early treatise on the weather and other natural phenomena. And yes, it's the reason why the study of weather is called "meteorology" to this day—the Greek *metéōros* just meant "high in the air," and to Aristotle, shooting stars and thunderstorms were all part of the same system. That theory didn't age well, but elsewhere in *Meteorologica* he got the spherical-Earth thing right, some 1,800 years before all that New World stuff. In your face, Columbus!

3. Don't be silly, of course "Graea" is not how we got our "gray." That one came from Proto-Germanic, which evolved its vocabulary wholly separate from the Greco-Roman tradition. Have you hugged a lexicographer today?

Romans came to see their empire as a supermodern update to the Greek way of doing things, but it's still probably coincidence that they picked *Graeci* as their name for that whole civilization. Accidental burn!

In any case, there are quite a few English expressions that would be way worse if you swapped in "Hellenic" for "Greek":

- **Greek gift**, meaning "something given with treacherous purpose." Naturally, it refers to the Trojan horse myth, which is first attested in Homer's eighth-century B.C.E. epic *The Odyssey*…and was apparently forgotten some 1,100 years later, when a Bible commentary by St. Jerome gave us the proverb "Don't look a gift horse in the mouth."
- **Fenugreek**, literally "Greek hay," that nice-smelling and oh-so-versatile herb, touted by the alt-medicine crowd as a treatment for baldness, beriberi, boils, bronchitis, cancer, cellulitis, chapped lips, constipation, diabetes, dysmenorrhea, eczema, erectile dysfunction, fever, flesh wounds, gout, hernia, high cholesterol, inflammation, kidney troubles, leg ulcers, low sex drive, lymph pain, mouth ulcers, muscle pain, obesity, ovarian cysts, Parkinson's disease, tuberculosis, and weak lactation. Ask your doctor!
- **Greek fire**, that mysterious petroleum-based weapon that the Byzantine Empire used to immolate enemy ships by setting ablaze the surface of the ocean itself, thus fending off invaders for nearly eight hundred years. Intentional burn!

By the way, there was a second path to this Duh answer: through "Parnas," short for holy Mount Parnassus. But that might have called to mind *The Imaginarium of Doctor Parnassus*, that 2009 film by Terry Gilliam remembered, if at all, as the last filmed appearance of Heath Ledger. And *that* might have bummed you out, so aren't you glad you didn't go that way?

—C.D.S.

Q. Kate Middleton's wedding bouquet contained the flower *Dianthus barbatus*, otherwise known as sweet what?

A. William.

As you might expect in a country where they still reenact the Battle of Hastings nearly a millennium later, most every bit of plant life at the wedding of the Duke and Duchess of Cambridge[1] was chosen for some other reason than just looking pretty. Sweet William is an obvi-dorable reference to Kate's husband, but her all-white bouquet also contained a sprig of myrtle, which has appeared in the wedding flowers of nearly every British royal bride since Queen Victoria planted a bush on the Isle of Wight in 1845.

Wills and Kate got hitched on Arbor Day 2011, so naturally they filled Westminster Abbey with English trees: field maples and hornbeams, respectively symbolizing humility and resilience. In true conservationist fashion, the trees came in pots, and were left afterward to be planted at Llwynywermod, the yes-it's-Welsh estate where Prince Charles sometimes hangs.

Back to her person, the lace on Kate's Alexander McQueen gown featured four types of plants, representing the British Isles—roses for England, plus:

- **Thistles** for Scotland. This prickly plant has been a symbol of the Scots since at least the reign of James III, who was indeed unloved: James was killed in 1488, in the *second* major rebellion of his reign.

---

1. On that happy day, the couple picked up three new sets of titles: one English (Duke and Duchess of Cambridge), one Scottish (Earl and Countess of Strathearn), and one Northern Irish (when Kate's in Derry, they call her Lady Carrickfergus, which is way easier to say than "the Baroness of Carrickfergus").

- **Daffodils** for Wales. We agree that this was a much better choice for the gown than that *other* Welsh horticultural symbol, the leek, unless the duchess was planning to make soup afterward.
- **Shamrocks** for Ireland, duh.

For pure plant game, though, Kate has nothing on Meghan Markle,[2,3] who in 2018 married William's little brother, Prince Harry. Her wedding gown was famously devoid of ornamentation, but the veil was a botanical *tour de force*: it featured a different flower for each of the fifty-three nations of the British Commonwealth, plus poppies for her home state of California. As far as we know, there's no flower called the "Hot Harry," so Markle couldn't directly represent her groom in the bouquet, but she *did* carry forget-me-nots—the favorite flower of Harry's late mother, Diana—and winter sweet, from in front of the home they shared. Aww.

Oh, there was myrtle in Meghan's bouquet too. We're not sure what happens if you're marrying into the royal family and you hate myrtle, but it seems a safe bet that Victoria would not be amused.

—S.D.Z.

2. The British royal family isn't exactly known for inclusiveness, but the Duchess of Sussex may not be the very first person of color to marry in. One pervasive historical rumor suggests that George III's wife, Charlotte Sophia of Mecklenburg-Strelitz, had black ancestors on both sides. True or not, it's certainly the case that George chose his bride, sight unseen, by ordering a survey of all eligible German Protestant noblewomen. *Wie romantisch!*

3. In our opinion, "Duchess of Sussex" is even harder to say than "Baroness of Carrickfergus," and even "Mecklenburg-Strelitz"—but go on, try them all for yourself! Preferably in a public place.

Q. How many stars are on the Texas flag?

A. One.

The short version: as part of the larger Mexican state Coahuila y Tejas, its flag had two stars. When Texas rebelled in 1836, they took their star with them, because...you know, Texas.

The way longer version: there's a reason why the Texas flag looks so much like Chile's "La Estrella Solitaria"—which, yes, also means "The Lone Star." Let's do it!

Born in 1750, Francisco de Miranda was one of those Enlightenment guys, like Franklin, Jefferson, and Lafayette, dedicated to spreading (literally) revolutionary ideas all across the Atlantic. After a trans-European education, Miranda went full-bore into the French Revolution, and he brought that spirit back for an ultimately failed liberation campaign in his native Venezuela.[1]

En route, in 1805, he tried to muster support from US Secretary of State James Madison, who played against I-wrote-the-Bill-of-Rights type by pleading the Neutrality Act. But later, as president, Madison got swept up in New World revolution fever after all, and posted a South American consul who eventually helped out with Chile's 1810s independence struggle, the drafting of its first constitution, and reportedly even the design of

---

1. Well, kinda-failed. After two quickly extinguished tries at a republican government, they finally won lasting independence under Simón Bolívar in 1821. Nowadays, they're a very healthy nation, inspiring such BBC headlines as "Venezuela crisis: 'People are ready to explode,'" and "Venezuela crisis: What is happening?"

its new flag[2]—the same liber-tacular colors as the US and French ones, with a single white star evoking an earlier flag of the native Mapuche people.

Back in Texas, we now catch up with one David G. Burnet, whom Miranda had recruited for the Venezuelan thing in that same fateful US visit. As Texas's interim president after their revolution, Burnet approved a solid blue flag with a lone gold star. But between Native American wars and the constant Mexican re-invasion threat, nobody wanted to move to the Republic of Texas, and by 1839 they were in full statehood-seeking mode. During that courtship, they adopted the current flag—decades later, there was still no better Enlightenment branding than the good ol' red, white, and blue.

After six years of wooing, Texas finally got annexed in 1845. Burnet was appointed as its first secretary of state—perhaps a slight underachievement for a guy whose middle name was Gouverneur.[3] To recap:

- A Venezuelan influenced an American.
- That American influenced some Chileans.
- Those Chileans influenced a Texan, who helped change the flag so he could suck up to America.

The sucking up was short-lived, of course. Texans were big-time slavers, who would eventually bone America's whole balance of power. The Stars and Stripes flew in Austin for a measly sixteen years before being (briefly) supplanted by the Stars and Bars.

They're all cool now, though.

—A.R.

2. The consul, Joel R. Poinsett, made a career as a south-of-the-border buttinsky. As minister to Mexico, he once essentially tried to redraw the border without Mexico noticing (they did). They even coined the word *poinsettismo* for his a-hole interloping. But he brought back a nice Christmas gift for American gardeners: a red, winter-blooming flower that's still called the poinsettia.

3. It didn't help when Burnet picked a campaign fight with beloved war hero Sam Houston, whom he labeled "Big Drunk" and an opium addict. In turn, Houston called Burnet a hog thief. Houston won that election for the Texas presidency, and blocked payment of Burnet's VP paycheck.

Q. What is the state bird of Maryland?

A. The Baltimore oriole.

You know the oriole (*Icterus galbula*). It's got an orange belly, black head and wings, its wingspan is about a foot, and it weighs about an ounce. Its breeding range covers most everything east of the Rockies. Apart from the distinctive colors, it is exactly like any bird you're likely to picture when you think of the word *bird*.

So, let's talk baseball!

By the time the state bird was chosen in 1947, Baltimore had already been home to four baseball teams called the Orioles—two in the minors and two in the majors.[1] But the current Orioles franchise started its major-league life in 1901 as the Milwaukee Brewers, sixty-nine years before another team took the same name (after moving—after one season in Seattle).

The O.G. Brewers moved in 1902 and became the St. Louis Browns (yes, after one big-league season—owners, right?). For decades they shared Sportsman's Park with the Cardinals, who once bested their landlords in a 1944 World Series played, conveniently, all at that one location.

The next few years weren't kind, though, and in two short seasons as owner, future Hall of Famer Bill Veeck made the hapless Browns of the early fifties a mecca for bizarre promotional antics. For one game he assigned

---

1. After two seasons in Maryland, one of those two teams moved to the Bronx (seriously, owners), eventually calling themselves the Yankees. The first four of their twenty-seven World Series titles were keyed by beloved Baltimore orphan George "Babe" Ruth.

field-management duties to crowd consensus; for another he signed show-biz dwarf Eddie Gaedel for one pinch-hitting appearance.[2]

Since finally settling in Baltimore after Veeck cashed out in 1953, the Orioles have won three World Series, raked in five American League MVP and six Cy Young Awards, and once hosted a game with zero paying spectators.[3]

There are five Baseball Hall of Fame players enshrined in Orioles caps, including:

- **Eddie Murray**, who struck out 104 times in his 1977 Rookie of the Year campaign. For the hundredth, his teammates broke out champagne.
- **Cal Ripken Jr.**, brother of Billy Ripken, who once appeared on a baseball card with a bat whose knob very legibly read "FUCK FACE."
- **Frank Robinson**, a civil rights activist who was described in his playing days by *The Sporting News* as a "Grade-A Negro"—and eventually proved it, by becoming MLB's first black manager in 1975. Still, that wasn't a very nice way to say that.

—C.D.S.

2. The 43-inch Gaedel was walked on four pitches and lifted for a pinch runner who did not score, in a game the Browns lost 6–2, in a season they finished with 102 losses. The man he replaced in the lineup that day, right fielder Frank Saucier, collected exactly one base hit in a big-league career that lasted sixty-four days. One assumes this series of transactions didn't burnish Veeck's Hall of Fame credentials as much as the 1947 season, when he signed Larry Doby to the Indians, thus breaking the American League's color barrier.

3. It was April 2015, the city was in a state of emergency thanks to police-brutality protests, and the Orioles beat the White Sox 8–2. First baseman Chris Davis flipped several baseballs into the empty stands. As always, "Thank God I'm a Country Boy" was played during the seventh-inning stretch. (Just by the way, Baltimore is not rural, and John Denver never lived there.)

Q. Who was the first US president with a middle name?

A. John Quincy Adams.

He also served in the Massachusetts Senate, the US House *and* Senate, the cabinet, and nearly the Supreme Court,[1] and was minister to four different countries, including the UK right after the War of 1812. A critic of party politics, he nonetheless threw in with the Federalists, the Democratic-Republicans, the National Republicans, the Anti-Masonics (seriously), and the Whigs. In his spare time, he was a practicing lawyer, a Harvard professor, and a fluent speaker of seven languages. When John F. Kennedy sat down with a ghostwriter to produce his Pulitzer-winning book, *Profiles in Courage*, the only president on the list was his homeboy J.Q.

We need a break after just *typing* all that.

Born in 1767—next door to the birthplace of his dad, second president John Not-Quincy Adams[2]—J.Q.'s life didn't take long to get interesting. At age seven he went with his mother Abigail to check out the action at Bunker Hill (from a safe distance). At ten, on a transatlantic trip with his father, his ship was attacked by British vessels, hit by a hurricane, and struck by lightning, killing four (total).

After seeing war and death firsthand as a child, Adams became a diplomat and was involved in many peace treaties:

1. James Madison nominated him in 1811, and the Senate even confirmed him, but he declined so he could focus on his diplomatic career. Sure enough, he served as a foreign minister for all five presidents who preceded him.

2. J.Q.'s great-grandpa, John No-Middle-Name Quincy, was on his deathbed at the time. Quincy had been Speaker of the Massachusetts House; the part of Braintree where the Adamses were born was renamed Quincy in his honor. Seriously, they were all obnoxious overachievers.

- He was his dad's secretary during the **Treaty of Paris** negotiations that formally ended the American Revolution. In France he saw the Montgolfier brothers demonstrate their new hot-air balloon. Adams wrote that the flight was heralded with cannon fire—hopefully in the other direction.
- In 1814 Adams headed America's **Treaty of Ghent** delegation, ending the War of 1812. Andrew Jackson got a big career boost[3] at the Battle of New Orleans—fought after the treaty was signed in Belgium, but before news reached the US. Oopsie!
- The **Transcontinental Treaty** was "perhaps the greatest victory ever won by a single man in the diplomatic history of the United States," according to *Britannica*. It extended the country all the way to the Pacific—and by bringing Florida into the US, it was also America's biggest comedic victory.

In 1824 Adams was elected president. The main highlights of his single term: skinny-dipping in the Potomac every morning and allegedly getting a pet alligator from the Marquis de Lafayette, which he kept in a White House bathtub to scare unsuspecting guests. Naturally, he couldn't stop himself from signing some more treaties, so he did that too.

After *that*, he spent seventeen years stumping for emancipation in Congress—a House colleague called him "the archest enemy of Southern slavery that ever existed." Still all fire-bellied, he was speaking out against the Mexican-American War when he suffered a fatal stroke in 1848. Fittingly, his funeral committee included a freshman senator from Illinois named Abraham Lincoln.

—M.S.

---

3. Jackson was Adams's presidential opponent in 1824. He had a plurality of the electoral college, but two spoiler candidates kept him under 50 percent, and the House picked Adams. Jackson prevailed in the 1828 rematch, and…you know, ask the Cherokee how that worked out.

Q. Brooks Brothers hand-stitched "One Country, One Destiny" into a custom-made coat worn by what US president?

A. Abraham Lincoln.

Brooks Brothers celebrated its bicentennial in 2018, exhibiting remarkable staying power for any commercial business. But that shouldn't be so surprising: ready-to-wear suits pretty much didn't exist until they introduced them in 1849, and who hates upscale convenience?

Now a subsidiary of the evocatively named Retail Brand Alliance, the company is quick to let you know that forty US presidents have donned its duds—both dudes involved in 2017's awkward torch-passing, as well as:

- **Franklin D. Roosevelt**, who somehow managed to pull off a collared cape and fedora combo at the Yalta Conference without looking like a vampire hunter.[1]
- His distant cousin, macho dandy **Teddy Roosevelt**, who had many of his military uniforms tailored by Brooks Brothers. And you know how he loved his military uniforms.
- **John F. Kennedy**, who was wearing one of their shirts when he was assassinated. They, uh, don't advertise that part.

Another piece of assassination-wear, Lincoln's frock coat *is* something BB crows about, and for obvious reasons: it's superfancy, he's as famous as ever, and it's good to know they can accommodate the gangly among us. But of

---

1. Many FDR conspiracy theories revolve around his membership in the Shriners, a semi-secret society that runs twenty-two children's hospitals, while perhaps being dressed by kids as well. Compared to their ghastly trademark fez, the Yalta vampire-hunter look is timelessly chic.

all people, it's interesting that Lincoln wasn't bothered by the fact they played both sides of the line. In some slave-owning families, it was a status symbol to put such a high-class brand on their domestics, and New York clothiers happily obliged with special "livery" departments. Brooks Brothers has never publicly acknowledged its part in the slave trade—you certainly won't find it in the extensive corporate history on their website—but they were signatories to the 1853 op-ed "The Tailor's Appeal," which was pretty much a bitchfest about Southern merchants not paying their bills. Surprise!

Once Honest Abe was in office, they played it straight, right? Well… In 1861, Brooks Brothers filled 36,000 Union army uniform orders, including a batch of 300 for then-quartermaster Chester A. Arthur. But contracts were usually awarded based on the highest bribes, and clothiers frequently cut serious corners to deliver the massive orders: ill-fitting uniforms missing buttons and buttonholes, glued-together uniforms of decaying fabric that disintegrated in the rain, shoe soles made of wood chips, and non-regulation cloth colors that caused actual incidents of friendly fire.

All these crappy clothes were heavily marked up for governments—regular army as well as state militias—which in turn made soldiers pay for their own uniforms. And yes, Brooks Brothers was part of the gross profiteering; a contemporary account called their goods "shoddy, poor sleazy stuff,[2] woven open enough for sieves, and then filled with shearman's dust." When asked why he didn't lower prices to match the costs on the inferior rags he was pushing, Elisha Brooks replied, "I cannot ascertain the difference without spending more time than I can now devote to that purpose."[3]

But still—forty presidents! Pretty cool, right?

—J.H.G.

---

2. Indeed, the new-ish "shoddy" became something of a catchphrase at the time. No one knows the etymology for sure, but we'd just like to point out that it's one vowel sound away from…you know, a certain vulgar synonym.

3. In his defense, dolphin-jumping through piles of money, Scrooge McDuck–style, is pretty time-consuming.

Q. Upon taking power in Cuba, Fidel Castro ordered the nationwide destruction of what board game?

A. Monopoly.

Inspired by the seminal Progressive economist Henry George, who proposed abolishing all taxes save a steep levy on rich landowners, in 1903 stenographer Lizzie Magie created the The Landlord's Game.[1] Like modern Monopoly, it had a hollow-square board, Chance cards, and the goal of acquiring a whole mess of money and property. Unlike Monopoly, players could opt into a George-inspired "single tax" rule, wherein rent gets paid into a public treasury that's used to fund free education and generally create wealth for everyone.

The idea was that folks would play both ways, and realize that the single tax system was morally superior—but, then as now, Americans preferred windpipe-crushing to fellow-feeling. When Parker Brothers published Charles Darrow's suspiciously similar game Monopoly in 1935,[2] they scrapped the single tax option, and papered over Magie's originating role as well. Only in the 1970s was the real story dug up, by a professor suing Parker Brothers for the right to create—wait for it—a game called Anti-Monopoly.

Somehow, none of this progressive past meant a damned thing when Fidel Castro came to power in 1959. By then Monopoly had a devoted following in Cuba—along with a local rip-off version, Capitolio—so Castro ordered

1. Working women were pretty rare back then, but Lizzie was totally self-sufficient and a committed first-wave feminist. As a burn on marriage, she once took out a joke personal ad offering herself for sale as a "young woman American slave." This wasn't even a college art project.

2. Yes, Monopoly came out in the midst of the Great Depression—which, you'll recall, was immediately preceded by a period of huge wealth inequality. Never change, America.

every copy destroyed as part of his island-wide purge on all things imperialist. To further solidify his anti-capitalist cred, he also seized and nationalized a bunch of American-owned oil refineries, offering not a single peseta of compensation. Never ones to waste a good grudge, the US spent the next forty years plotting Fidel's destruction through increasingly silly means, including:

- Arming his disgruntled mistress with poison pills. She got cold feet, not that it mattered—she'd stashed them in some cold cream, which rendered them unusable. Castro guessed her intentions anyway, and straight-up handed the woman his gun and dared her to shoot him. The flustered paramour boinked him instead, and somewhere, Sean Connery did that ooky Sean Connery grin.
- Exploiting Castro's love of scuba diving, either by lining his wet suit with deadly bacterial spores or planting a booby-trapped seashell at his favorite swimming spot.[3] Haven't you guys heard of shark pheromones?
- Spiking his radio studio with a spray of LSD-style psychotropics. Perhaps the CIA had been reading early-sixties anti-drug pamphlets and assumed taking hallucinogens would make *El Presidente* leap from a building or pull his own head off.

All these schemes were for naught, and Ol' Beardo escaped the estimated six hundred assassination plots with nary a scratch. He ruled Cuba until 2006, and passed "Go" via natural causes a decade later—blissfully oblivious, it would seem, to the irony that he had for so long held such a monopoly on power.

—E.K.

---

3. Castro loved diving so much, and was so (justifiably) antsy about assassination attempts, that he sectioned off part of the gorgeous reef Jardines de la Reina as his own personal scuba-scape. Nowadays, it's one of the longest stretches of the Caribbean not ravaged by pollution. Thanks, paranoia!

Q. The birthday of ex-slave and abolitionist leader Frederick Douglass is in what month?

A. February.

As Chris Rock so aptly pointed out, "Black History Month is in the shortest month of the year, and the coldest—just in case we want to have a parade." In fact, it didn't become a full month until 1970; Negro History *Week* was started in 1926, by *The Journal of Negro History* founder Carter G. Woodson, to coincide with the birthdays of both Frederick Douglass and Abraham Lincoln.

In any case, Douglass is way more interesting than Black History Month.[1] So here's the rundown: Frederick Augustus Washington Bailey was born into slavery on a Maryland plantation in February of 1818.[2] He escaped in 1838 on an actual railroad to New York and immediately joined the burgeoning abolitionist movement.

This may sound like standard stuff so far, but most details of Douglass's life read like tall tales—and they're far too numerous for a three-point bullet list. He paid white children with bread to help teach him to read, then taught other slaves, up to forty at a time. He was photographed more times than any nineteenth-century American, just because he thought photography humanized black people. He raised black troops for the Union army, then campaigned against Lincoln's reelection in 1864 for not supporting the enfranchisement of freed black men. He was the first black nominee

1. As the thing you almost certainly picture when you hear his name, Douglass's hair alone may be more interesting than Black History Month.

2. Maybe. There was no written record, so Frederick just picked February 14 as his birthday. He also picked his own surname, from a Walter Scott poem a friend was reading. You may *think* of yourself as self-made; Frederick Douglass *was* self-made.

for vice president, on the first ticket to nominate a woman.[3] He married Helen Pitts, a white abolitionist daughter of abolitionists, whose parents nonetheless disowned her for it.

In his later years, a rightly famous Douglass was often invited to work for various presidents:

- **Ulysses S. Grant** sent him to what is now the Dominican Republic to see if the US should annex it. Douglass wanted to, but we didn't.
- **Rutherford B. Hayes** made him the first black US marshal, allowing him to expand government job opportunities for black workers.
- **Benjamin Harrison** sent Douglass back to Hispaniola, appointing him as minister to Haiti. Douglass resigned after the administration tried to bully Haiti out of a spot for a new naval base.

But Douglass's greatest legacy comes from having been a forceful writer, in an era when writing mattered a lot. His three autobiographies were bestsellers from the 1840s through the 1880s, and are still widely read today. His newspaper, *The North Star*, advanced the cause of abolitionism for a broad national audience. Not too bad for someone who paid for his schooling with baked goods.

Incidentally, he printed *The North Star* on a press purchased by his supporters in Ireland and England, who treated him not "as a color, but as a man." Treating him as a month? Not sure what they would have made of that.

—S.B.

---

3. It was 1872, and the Equal Rights Party nominated him alongside presidential candidate Victoria Woodhull. An early superfeminist, Douglass was also the only black person, man or woman, at the 1848 Seneca Falls Convention.

Q. What was the last name of the guy who took his arrest to the Supreme Court in 1963 because the cops didn't tell him his rights?

A. Miranda.

In March 1963, Ernesto Miranda was brought in by police on suspicion of rape and kidnapping. After being positively identified in a lineup—or so the less-than-honest cops told him—Miranda confessed to the crimes, without ever being informed of his Fifth Amendment right to remain silent. Convicted at trial, he hitched a ride with the American Civil Liberties Union Express all the way to the Supreme Court, which threw out the conviction in a landmark 1966 decision.

But you probably could have guessed that. *Miranda v. Arizona* is one of the few Supreme Court cases that most Americans can probably explain, whether they're familiar with the details or not. The warnings required by the case are drilled into the national consciousness from decades of *Law & Order*.[1] "You have the right to remain silent. Anything you say can and will be used against you in a court of law. You have the right to an attorney. If you cannot afford an attorney, one will be provided for you."

It's not that simple, though, as Miranda protections have been slowly whittled away in the decades since. In the 2010 *Berghuis v. Thompkins* decision, "swing justice" Anthony Kennedy wrote that in order for Miranda rights to actually apply, the accused must *explicitly state out loud* that they are invoking their right to remain silent. Merely *remaining* silent? Not

---

1. As of this writing, binge-watching every episode of every series in the franchise would require more than thirty-five days of round-the-clock viewing. Make sure you've got a big bucket by the couch.

good enough.[2] Mind you, the *Miranda* ruling sparked controversy from the minute it was handed down:

- In his dissent, Justice Byron White predicted that countless violent criminals would re-offend, after being returned to "the environment which produced" them. Remember, kids, the only *really* safe place is jail!
- In the Omnibus Crime Control and Safe Streets Act of 1968—first conceived five years earlier, after the JFK assassination—Congress effectively overturned *Miranda*. With police departments wary of all the constitutional ambiguity, though, they kept on reading the rights, and the Supreme Court wasn't forced to uphold its decision until *Dickerson v. United States* in 2000 (it did).
- In 2002, lawyers for the infamous "American Taliban" John Walker Lindh claimed US agents had conducted coercive interrogations without Mirandizing him. But on the day the confession-suppression hearing was to start, Lindh changed his plea to guilty, leaving legal journals to ponder what might have been.

Miranda himself made a handy example for people who'd like to reverse his namesake decision. He was retried without the confession in evidence, convicted again, and sentenced to twenty to thirty years. Paroled after ten, he did another year after *breaking* parole[3] and shortly thereafter, in 1976, was fatally stabbed in a bar fight at age thirty-four.

As far as we know, Fifth Amendment rights don't extend to the afterlife.

—T.C.

---

2. Bottom line: get a lawyer. Even if you're sure you haven't done anything wrong, the only words coming out of your facehole should be "I want a lawyer, and I will not answer questions until I have one." And no, reading this book doesn't count as consulting a lawyer. *Get a lawyer!*

3. In the meantime, he turned lemons to lemonade, selling autographed Miranda warning cards for $1.50 each. That's probably the most American thing in this story.

Q. America's first kindergarten had its classes taught in what language?

A. German.

Neglected as a child, and fitfully seeking employment as a young adult, in 1805 a preacher's kid named Friedrich Froebel took a teaching job in Frankfurt. He quickly recognized his calling, and jumped from school to school in Switzerland and modern-day Germany, developing his theory that in order to flourish, children need permission to express themselves, and lots of individual and group playtime. In 1837 he opened his own school in Prussia, which he called the Child Nurture and Activity Institute—before settling on the much pithier "Garden of Children." Soon enough, thanks to the kindergarten movement, Germany was the only place in the Western world where children under six were being educated.

In the 1840s, Margarethe Meyer heard Froebel speak in her hometown of Hamburg and was smitten with his ideas. By the time she'd run off to London following a failed revolution, married fellow exile Carl Schurz,[1] had a couple kids, and emigrated with a wave of the liberal German bourgeoisie to Watertown, Wisconsin, Margarethe was ready to open her own kindergarten in 1856. Three years after opening that kindergarten, Schurz chanced to meet Boston schoolteacher and prominent transcendentalist Elizabeth Peabody.[2] Another instant convert, Peabody

1. On his resume? Leading a Union division at Gettysburg, giving Joseph Pulitzer his first newspaper job, becoming the first German-born US senator, and editing the *New York Evening Post*.

2. On her resume? Being the first female American book publisher and the first American of any gender to translate Buddhist scripture. She also published Thoreau's essay "Civil Disobedience," and it's not really an accomplishment, but we can't *not* tell you that her brothers-in-law were Nathaniel Freaking Hawthorne and Horace Freaking Mann.

opened the first English-speaking kindergarten; traveled to Germany to study with Froebel's protégé, the magnificently named Baroness von Marenholtz-Bülow; founded a magazine called the *Kindergarten Messenger*; and lobbied Congress to make kindergarten free for all American kids. She died in 1893, a year after the establishment of the International Kindergarten Union.

Of course, Froebel and Schurz weren't the only Europeans to innovate in early-childhood education:

- In 1912 the Austrian spiritualist **Rudolf Steiner** created anthroposophy, which he called "a path from the mind and spirit in the human being, to the mind and spirit in the cosmos." Which, okay—but he also founded the Waldorf School, which purports to cultivate students' "intellectual, emotional, physical, and spiritual capacities" through immersion in the arts. Sounds good to us!
- Coming-of-age in Fascist Italy, **Loris Malaguzzi** took a teacher-training course during the Second World War, then developed his teaching philosophy in a little school near the North Italian town that gave it a name: Reggio Emilia teachers thoroughly document everything the kids talk about, then review it to find out what they're truly interested in, and tailor the activities that way.[3]
- Already the first Italian woman to graduate from medical school, **Maria Montessori** later became probably the best-known of European early-childhood educators. She studied the educational challenges of children with mental disabilities, then in 1906 she applied her theories on creative potential to kids without disabilities. By supplying tactile materials for self-directed learning, Montessori created a vaguely snooty system of preschool education that's been replicated worldwide.

—C.D.S.

3. If our kids were in that program, there would be a lot of activities revolving around using superpowers to get revenge on bad guys—but come to think of it, that *does* sound engaging.

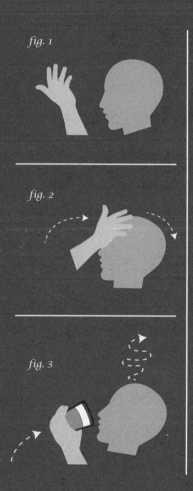

fig. 1

fig. 2

fig. 3

6

A WORLD

OF PAIN

Q. Most of the Hollywood Walk of Fame runs along what street?

A. Hollywood Boulevard.

Stanley Kramer may not be a household name, but every year millions of people look down on him.

By 1960, as a producer, Kramer already had three Best Picture Oscar nominations to his name. His latest movie in the director's chair—*Inherit the Wind*, about the 1925 Scopes Monkey Trial—would open around the US in November to widespread acclaim. And so, after someone at the Hollywood Chamber of Commerce had the bright idea to embed bronze stars in granite tiles—and after a two-year delay caused by *de rigueur* lawsuits—Kramer's became the first name on the Walk of Fame.[1]

As it's done for six decades now, the Walk was launched to draw tourists to the glitzy-glammy side of Hollywood while distracting them from, you know, the hookers and stuff. If we go all the way back to the 1880s, though, the neighborhood was just getting white-people-settled as an agricultural suburb of Los Angeles by fig-farming developers Harvey and Daeida Wilcox. They turned out to be better developers than farmers, and soon they were subdividing their ranch into a small town with all the amenities, including a trolley that traveled up and down—where else?—Hollywood Boulevard.[2]

1. This, despite the fact that he was not even in the first class of nominees selected in 1958. That octet included Joanne Woodward, Burt Lancaster, and a bunch of more obscure people. A natural media magnet who already had her Oscar for *The Three Faces of Eve*, Woodward was *also* the one in the widest-published photos, and so culture has sometimes misremembered her as the first on the Walk overall. She wasn't. Now you know.

2. Where's the Hollywood sign in this history? A real-estate developer built a big ad for "Hollywoodland" in the 1920s. It fell into ruin, and the "land" part got taken down. Of all people, Hugh Hefner renovated the rest with some rich friends in the 1970s. And, scene.

It wasn't until the 1910s that movie studios started popping up. Noted Jersey buttface Thomas Edison kept suing anyone on the East Coast who tried to make movies with any sort of patent-violating equipment, which to him just meant basically any equipment whatsoever. It was harder to serve papers to someone from 3,000 miles away back then,[3] so the industry decamped to L.A. and happened to cluster in Hollywood. Early comers included D.W. Griffith, Cecil B. DeMille, and Charlie Chaplin, all titans represented by bronze stars today (even the super-racist one).

While a Walk star is often thought of as a lifetime achievement award, they're usually awarded right at the peak of celebrity, meaning the 2,600-plus stars are about as rare as magazine covers—they lay about two stars per month these days. It also makes the Walk a sort of living time capsule. Consider the honorees in the sixtieth-anniversary year of 2018:

- **RuPaul**, whose star-laying ceremony emphasized over and over that he's the Walk's first drag queen. Because there were so many other contenders for that claim.
- *Hamilton*'s **Lin-Manuel Miranda**, who is, as we speak, probably gathering guest rappers for a concept album/movie about his ceremony.
- Galaxy guardian **Zoe Saldana** and O.G. Wonder Woman **Lynda Carter**, representing our total obsession with cape movies…and the fact that occasionally they have women in them!

—L.M.P.

3. Even harder if they ducked out to Mexico—a common occurrence in the early days, as legend has it.

Q. What is the world's second-tallest mountain?

A. K2.

You *might* call it Mount Godwin-Austen or Chhogori, but to virtually everyone on Earth, this remote and terrifying thing is just K2. That's thanks to the Great Trigonometrical Survey, in which nineteenth-century Britons calculated the cosine of theta, or some crap like that, to figure out that Everest (named for Surveyor General George Everest) was the tallest mountain in the world.

The second peak measured in the Karakoram range, K2 was tersely labeled along with the others because they didn't know the local names yet. It turned out that K1 was called Masherbrum, and K3–K5 were different parts of Gasherbrum. That second mountain was the only one that didn't have a name,[1] and so K2 stuck.[2]

Of course, once they found this ridiculously high, steep thing, people started trying to climb it. In 1902 an expedition including yes-that-Satanist Aleister Crowley got to 21,407 feet—over 6,800 short, guys! In 1909 Luigi Amedeo, Duke of the Abruzzi, found the correct route on the East Ridge but couldn't make it up the whole way. In 1954 two other Italians finally

---

1. That's because *it's not visible from any inhabited location.* It's on the China-Pakistan border, not far from their tripoint with India—hardly a cosmopolitan part of the world. A local climbing organization advertises a trip to K2 that takes two days by bus, then two by Jeep, then eight by camel. Pack a lunch!

2. Later geographers tried to name it for Everest's coworker Henry Haversham Godwin-Austen, but this was rejected even by the imperialist Royal Geographical Society. While we're at it, Chhogori ("big mountain") is a spurious Balti name that may have been made up sarcastically on the spot. Nowadays, even locals go with "Ketu."

did become the first climbers to reach the top and helped to ensure that the most popular route would forever be called the Abruzzi Spur.

The summit shares a high fatality rate with several other tough mountains of legend, including:

- Nearby **Nanga Parbat**, whose name comes from the Sanskrit for "naked mountain" but is better known as the "killer mountain" for obvious reasons. Heinrich Harrer planned to climb it on behalf of Hitler but was arrested by Britons, eventually escaped, and then became the Dalai Lama's tutor. If that sounds like the plot of *Seven Years in Tibet*, that's because it literally is.
- **Annapurna**, in the Himalayas, is an 8,000-meter-plus peak with the world's highest fatality rate. Its name means "replete with food," which is hilarious because it's way too high for anything to grow on it besides terror.
- **Kangchenjunga**, also in the Himalayas, is the third-highest mountain in the world. Nobody who climbs it actually goes to the *very* top because of a promise made to the local rulers to leave it pristine. See? They *can* show restraint!

But K2 is the northernmost of the ultra-tall Asian peaks; unlike the others, it's never been climbed in winter. There are seriously difficult segments in the 8,000-meter-plus "Death Zone," including a steep bottleneck that can cave in on either side—it claimed eleven lives in August 2008 alone.

In all, while more than three hundred people have made it to the top, seventy-seven have died trying. The point is, don't climb K2—and *especially* don't be like Polish death-wish-haver Andrzej Bargiel, who climbed up without oxygen in 2018, and then skied down the thing.[3]

—S.B.

3. Naturally, this was sponsored by Red Bull, which seems to have some sort of desire to destroy its entire customer base.

Q. Hoosier Hill is the highest point in what state?

A. Indiana.

On a clear, hot day in July 1936, Arthur Harmon Marshall reached the highest point in Indiana—five times. "After visiting the three points shown on the Winchester quadrangle as 1,240 feet," he wrote in his journal, "and also two other points called the highest by residents nearby, I feel sure I was on the summit of Indiana, but I don't know where it is."[1] Marshall needed to be certain, because at *some* point that day he became the first person ever to ascend the highest points of all forty-eight United States.[2]

A telegrapher by trade, the Pennsylvania native's high-pointer career started with a two-day ascent of Washington's Mount Rainier in 1919, the same week he'd been laid out for several days with rheumatism in his knees. Over the next few years, he set out bagging a few of the country's other most prominent mountains, with no particular goal in mind; it wasn't until 1930, after summiting Oregon's Mount Hood, New Hampshire's Mount Washington, and California's Mount Whitney, that he figured he might as well keep going. By 1935 he'd done all the hard ones, so that summer he collected fourteen high points, from Nebraska to Vermont. The next year

1. For the record, it's in Wayne County, near Winchester and the Ohio state line, and it's 1,257 feet above sea level. It's about 220 miles from the lowest point in Indiana—in the southwest, where the Wabash River flows into the Ohio. According to a math professor we asked, Hoosier Hill would have to be about 31,000 feet higher in order to see the low point from its "peak." Take that, flat-Earthers!

2. It's a good thing he didn't wait until 1959; he'd have had to tackle Mauna Kea (around 13,800 feet) and Denali (a lung-busting 20,310). Plus, he died in 1951, so that probably would have slowed him down.

he got *eighteen*, winding up…you know, somewhere in Indiana, which he called "last and most unsatisfactory."[3]

Nowadays, the real, honest-to-God high point is called Hoosier Hill—taken, of course, from the demonym for residents of Indiana, which you likely also remember as a 1986 film with an earnest Gene Hackman and a drunk Dennis Hopper. The word is as mysterious as it is cornpone, with the following dubious etymologies most often promulgated:

- When everyone had canal fever in the early nineteenth century, a contractor named Samuel Hoosier preferred Indiana workers—"Hoosier's men"—to Kentucky ones. We're not sure how to measure the best workers, but we'll just mention that today Kentucky consistently ranks among the bottom five states for adults with college degrees, and the top ten for obesity.
- Surveyors mapping the state often encountered squatters on the frontier, yelling out, "Who's here?" whenever they saw a smoking chimney. This was very likely *not* also the inspiration for "Who Is It," the top-twenty 1993 single by Gary native Michael Jackson.
- Settlers from northwest England wound up in the southern part of the state. They called themselves "hoozers," from the Cumbrian for "high hill," because Southern Indiana is the only topographically interesting bit…or maybe they just had a highly developed sense of sarcasm.

—C.D.S.

---

3. Pretty sure he was referring to the ambiguity, but it's also clear that all those lame high points didn't take too much out of his legs: on the way back to his home in Washington state, he took another trip to the top of Colorado's 14,440-foot Mount Elbert.

Q. Conjoined twins Chang and Eng Bunker were born in what country?

A. Siam.

Known since 1948 as Thailand, Siam is the geographic and cultural nougat core of Southeast Asia. From its 5-ton Golden Buddha statue at Wat Traimit[1] to Koh Phi Phi Leh, the island that upstaged Leo DiCaprio in *The Beach*, it'd very much be worthy of a long essay all its own…but the story of the Siamese twins is just too damned fascinating.

Chang and Eng were born without a surname in 1811, some 60 miles west of Bangkok. They emerged joined at the breastbone by a sinewy, arm-like ligament, to the horror of everyone but their unflappable mom. A very-much-flapped King Rama II ordered them executed as a bad omen[2]—but then promptly forgot his own edict and left them alone. Hooray for whimsically ineffective leaders!

When cholera took most of their family in 1819, the eight-year-old twins launched a successful fish-and-duck-egg business. By chance they met a Scottish trader, who mistook them at first for "some strange animal." He promised to make them stars on a brief tour of US and England, and after sailing away in 1829, they never saw their homeland again. How's that for a first act break?

---

1. To protect the statue from invaders, it was covered in stucco in the mid-1700s. The ruse held for two hundred years—until some clumsy movers dropped it, cracking the shell and revealing the gold within. How is this not a Nicolas Cage movie?

2. This bit aside, Rama II was a mostly chill king and a generous patron of poets. One of his favorites was Sunthorn Phu, a national hero despite (because of?) his years of jail time for illicit affairs and drunken brawling. Phu was later stripped of his salary for publicly nitpicking the poetry of the king's son, Rama III.

For the next few decades, the two toured off and on, holding Q&As for Western gawkers, and even inspiring an essay by a young Mark Twain. They settled in North Carolina, bought a bunch of farmland—and, less awesomely, more than a dozen slaves—and successfully applied for US citizenship, borrowing the Bunker name from a New York pal.

Dazzling the local social scene, they married a pair of non-twin sisters named Yates, despite their parents' misgivings and some intolerant towns-folk pelting their house with rocks. For a while the foursome shared a farm-house (and a bed), but eventually they split their estate and settled on a rotation: three days at Chang's house with Eng staying silent, then vice versa. Somehow, this bicameral romance worked: the two happy unions produced twenty-one children. Today, the Bunkers have over one thousand living descendants, including:

- **Caroline Shaw**, the youngest-ever Pulitzer Prize–winner in music. Among other things, she cowrote the Kanye West track "Wolves," featuring the Pulitzer-worthy line, "Who needs sorry when there's Hennessy?"
- **Alex Sink**, a former chief financial officer of Florida. Florida is the only state with a CFO, and is also home to a legendary 25-foot shark named Old Hitler.[3]
- Arizona archaeologist **Vance Haynes**, who coined the term "black mat" for a type of swamp soil. You thought they were all Indiana Jones?

Despite losing big on Confederate war bonds, the brothers held onto their huge estate until 1874, when Chang died in his sleep. Waking up attached to a corpse, an understandably panicked Eng cried, "Then I am going!" He died just a few hours after his brother, their official causes of death "blood clot" and "fright," respectively.

—E.K.

3. Seriously, Florida, never change.

Q. The Rockettes are based in a famous building that's part of what complex?

A. Rockefeller Center.

In 1922 the Tiller Girls left their home in Manchester, England, to bring their precision dance steps to Broadway's famed *Ziegfeld Follies*. Their founder, John Tiller (duh), had seen too many chorus lines ruined by sloppiness. The effect of Tiller's direction was evidently striking: one Russell Markert was in the audience, and he decided to start a leggier, higher-kicking American version. He took the urge for uniformity even further, hiring only women 62–66.5 inches tall.[1]

Markert's troupe debuted in 1925, and they were called…the Missouri Rockets. We may have forgotten to mention that Markert was visiting from St. Louis, and that's where he started the thing.

Eventually, he made his way back to New York, Rockets in tow, for a show at the Roxy Theatre. Their long-ass legs won the affection of audiences, and caught the attention of the owner, S.L. "Roxy" Rothafel[2] (duh). Roxy convinced Markert to keep a new line of dancers there, naturally renaming them…the Roxyettes. We're getting there!

Meanwhile, Rockefeller Center was being built in a formerly derelict Midtown neighborhood, by John D. Rockefeller Jr. (duh). This endeavor was a partnership between the Radio Corporation of America and Rothafel—who famously said, "Don't give the people what they want, give 'em something better," and by all accounts succeeded admirably. His new

---

1. Nowadays, a Rockette must be 66–70.5 inches tall. Inflation!

2. Originally from the German for "red apple." How could he *not* have been successful in New York?

"palace for the people" was called the Radio City Music Hall. It opened in 1932, with the Roxyettes performing a new dance number each week.[3] In 1934 they were finally and officially dubbed…the Rockettes.

Beyond their beautiful Art Deco confines, the ladies have spent the decades kicking their way to pop-culture ubiquity:

- During World War II, they were one of the very first USO acts. They even hosted a war-bond rally at Madison Square Garden, with Eleanor Roosevelt. No word on whether Eleanor joined the kick line.
- In 1955 they were on the premiere episode of NBC's crazy-ambitious live documentary series, *Wide Wide World*. Despite doing many things that had never been done before, the episode had one of history's most boring titles: "A Sunday in Autumn."
- In 2001 they danced down the steps of the Lincoln Memorial for George W. Bush's inauguration. No word on whether Donald Rumsfeld joined the kick line.

Nowadays, the eighty Rockettes—two troupes of forty each—are mostly a seasonal show, having started their Christmas Spectacular in 1933, and gracing the Macy's Thanksgiving Day Parade since 1957. During the busiest times, each dancer performs as many as 650 kicks per day.

As for Russell Markert, he died in 1990 at age ninety-one, leaving no surviving relatives. He was followed in death the next day by composer Aaron "Common Man" Copland, who got an entire half-page of obit copy in *The New York Times*.

Despite having led the Rockettes all the way up until 1971, Markert got less than half the space. Ain't that a kick in the head?

—L.T.

3. In fact, they performed up to five times a day, and sometimes slept at the theater—onsite facilities included a twenty-six-bed dormitory, a cafeteria, a tailor shop, and medical staff. One presumes foot rubs were on the menu.

Q. In English, the Greek word *philadelphia* usually translates to what two-word phrase?

A. Brotherly love.

Before he was a well-known Quaker agitator in America, William Penn was a well-known Quaker agitator in England. Just look at his 1668 pamphlet, *Truth Exalted*, which went so far as to call the Roman Catholic Church the "Whore of Babylon." Famed diary-keeper Samuel Pepys called this a "ridiculous nonsensical book" that he was "ashamed to read."[1]

Nor was Pepys the only hater. Penn got an early start as a rabble-rouser and was expelled from Oxford for refusing to participate in forced worship—which in turn caused his father to chase him out of their home with his cane. After typical disaffected-youth stints in Paris and law school, he finally got his act together, relatively speaking.

Always the rebel, though, Penn became a fervent Quaker at the exact moment when anti-Quaker sentiment was highest, and his participation got him both arrested and kicked out of his house several times. Penn's vocal minority religious beliefs even got him locked up in the Tower of London—in one case, right alongside the jury that had failed to convict him on street-preaching charges.[2]

Meanwhile, Will's father, *Sir* William Penn, had been a well-respected admiral in the Royal Navy and a member of the House of Commons. As

---

1. If you think *that's* salty, Pepys's diary quotes fellow Member of Parliament William Batten as having once said, "By God, I think the Devil shits Dutchmen."

2. The jurors sued and won, permanently winning UK juries independence from judges' opinions. England got its Toleration Act nineteen years later, in 1689—but it only covered Protestant Christians who believe in the Trinity. Baby steps!

he stared down death, Sir William worried what would happen to Junior when Dad wasn't there to protect him, so he pulled some strings to get the kid some colonial land, as the landed gentry do. Wisely turning his nose up at New Jersey, Will instead got the land that is now Pennsylvania—Charles II named it for the cool dead Penn, not the guy he was chasing out—and he lived there happily ever after.

Penn didn't come by himself though. Also known as the Society of Friends, his Quaker expat buddies were a bunch of peaceniks, who believed in the inherent potential for good in everyone. Naturally, they were reluctant to oppress other religious minorities in their new home, and they tried to make respectful trade and land deals with the indigenous Lenape people whose land they were now partly occupying. And when it came time to found a big city, Penn named it with the Greek words *philos* ("love") and *adelphos* ("brother").[3]

By far, Philly is not the only US city with an ironic translated name:

- **Indianapolis** is bastardized Greek for "city of Indians." According to the 2010 census, the Speedway city has a population that's 0.3 percent Native American.
- **Las Vegas** is Spanish for "the meadows." With Lake Mead now more than 130 feet below its water level in 2000, it's illegal for desert-bound Las Vegans to have grass in their front yards.
- Yup, **Los Angeles** is literally the City of Angels.

—N.H.

3. It would be another 286 years before the City of Brotherly Love pelted Santa Claus with snowballs—as though it's Santa's fault the city has such historically terrible weather and football.

Q. What's the only Canadian province that's completely disconnected from the North American mainland?

A. Prince Edward Island.

In 1864, delegates from the Maritime colonies got together in the tiny, sleepy capital of tiny, sleepy Prince Edward Island to talk about officially banding together. The Union army was on the verge of winning the American Civil War, and the British North Americans were worried the Yanks might celebrate their victory with a little bit of northerly invasion.

Though Charlottetown's inns were already booked up by a popular traveling circus, the conference *also* got cramped by some pushy delegates, bearing prodigious amounts of alcohol, from Ontario and Quebec (then forming the Province of Canada). Three years later, four hungover colonies became one drunken country.

Ironically, PEI was not one of those colonies. For a while it flirted with various options, including American statehood, before finally getting bribed into the confederation a few years later[1]—after British Columbia, Manitoba, and even the Northwest Territories, which to this day does not have enough people to be a province.

Anyway, since 1873, Canada has officially had federal jurisdiction over all three Maritimes:[2]

---

1. No, it wasn't with more booze. The weirder story: the tiny island had somehow gotten itself deep in railway debt, and Ottawa picked that up.

2. Newfoundland didn't join until *way* later, in 1949. But for reasons nobody entirely understands, it isn't counted among the Maritimes. Even in Canadian English, *maritime* is defined as "of, relating to, or bordering on the sea"; Newfoundland, one of the world's twenty biggest islands (and comprising some 30 percent of the modern province of Newfoundland and Labrador), would seem to qualify.

- **Nova Scotia**, the most populous of the three. It's also home to Halifax, the informal Maritime capital. With a bunch of universities and military bases, it's demographically younger than much of Canada, and is indeed a rocking metropolis…you know, by Maritime standards. It's got about 400,000 people.
- **New Brunswick**, the province you drive through to get to Nova Scotia. Here's a fun thing to do if you're American: the next time a Canuck is on your case about how little Americans know about the world, ask them for the capital of New Brunswick.[3]
- **Prince Edward Island**, but hopefully you already knew that.

PEI is the Rhode Island of Canada, its smallest province by a wide margin—but, unlike Rhode Island, it is an actual island. Odds are, if you've heard of the province at all, you know it for one of three things: red sand, potatoes, and…okay, you probably only know it from the Anne of Green Gables series.

But that's fine, because Anne is a big, big deal for PEI. Lucy Maud Montgomery's book was based on the real geography of Cavendish, which came in really handy when they wanted to build their tourism industry on it. There is even a real home called Green Gables; apart from the throngs of genteel visitors, you can recognize it from…the green gables, duh.

Right across the street you can also drop by Montgomery's home, where she wrote her books. She won't be there, mind you—in 1942, she was the guest of honor at a wake in the Green Gables farmhouse.

—P.S.P.

3. It's Fredericton. That took us a second too.

Q. What famous statue was uncovered in 1820 on the Greek island of Milos?

A. Venus de Milo.

Once upon a time, there was a French ensign named Olivier Voutier. He was digging for antiquities on the isle of Milos—then, like all of Greece, part of the Ottoman Empire—when a Greek farmer named Yorgos Kentrotas, who was just going about his business, found a statue with no arms that was otherwise, you know, pretty good.[1] Voutier wanted to keep it in French hands, so his officer friends concocted a plan to have it bought by the French ambassador, and then King Louis XVIII placed it in the Louvre. The end.

Of course, not all the pieces made it there. When the statue was dug up, it was in many fragments; *Venus*'s upper body wouldn't even stay on top of her lower body, until a hip piece was found that locked them together. To this day, the whereabouts of her arms remain a famous mystery—persistent legend has it that they were intentionally "misplaced" by the French because they were too rough, and would lessen the appeal.[2]

Indeed, most all of *Venus*'s vital statistics have been up for debate, starting with the actual subject of the statue (Venus was a Roman goddess, after all, not a Greek one).[3] Originally, the French fudged her age, claiming she

---

1. Well, Kentrotas thought it was *not* very good, because he was looking for stones to build a wall, and *Venus* is much too curvy. Voutier had to bribe him to keep digging.

2. They *really* wanted people to like her—they'd recently, embarrassingly, had to give back to Italy a well-loved similar statue, the *Venus de' Medici*, that they stole during the Napoleonic Wars.

3. So that would make her Venus's Greek counterpart, Aphrodite. Or maybe she's Amphitrite, the wife of Poseidon. Yet another theory claims that the statue is of some random prostitute. We think it looks a little bit like TV's Elisabeth Moss, but she wasn't born until 1982.

was from the Classical Greek period rather than the later, less esteemed Hellenistic Greece. We *are* at least sure of her height and weight—6 feet, 8 inches, and 3,000 pounds of pure chiseled marble. So, she's the same height as LeBron James, and about 2,750 more pounds. She could almost certainly back him down in the post—but taking the shot would be a problem. She has no arms, y'all.

Regardless of her provenance, *Venus's* popularity has not dwindled in the two centuries since she rose from the ground:

- In 1936 Salvador Dalí sculpted a cabinet-like version of the statue called *Venus de Milo with Drawers*. He also hosted weekly orgies, hung out with Alice Cooper, published a cookbook with aphrodisiacs in it, scammed Yoko Ono out of $10,000, filled a Rolls-Royce with 1,100 pounds of cauliflower, painted something called *Hitler Masturbating*, and believed he was the reincarnation of his own dead brother. But *Venus de Milo with Drawers* was pretty wacky too.
- On their landmark 1977 album *Marquee Moon*, in a song about love and/or drug abuse on the streets of New York, the band Television sang, "I fell right into the arms of Venus de Milo." They sketchily rhymed it with "feel low." Presumably the whole thing makes much more sense if you're in love and/or on drugs.
- In 2018 the Wonderful Pistachios people put her in modern clothes to shill their no-shell pistachios. They're "perfect for me," she said, "a woman without...a lot of time." Get it? She also *doesn't have arms*!

—M.S.

Q. Atlanta is sister cities with Tbilisi, the capital of what country?

A. Georgia.

During the Cold War, as Western rock moved from John Lennon and Lou Reed to Robert Plant and Joey Ramone, the Soviet Union officially noticed none of it. Sure, a few of the cool kids were trading hissy, umpteenth-generation bootleg tapes of albums from outside. But the Communist Party controlled the radio and the record-store inventories, and they only sanctioned square-ass "vocal-instrumental ensembles," with matching, weird-colored suits, and names like (seriously) The Jolly Fellows.

In March 1980, a few months before 45 percent of the world's nations boycotted the Moscow Olympics thanks to the USSR's Afghanistan adventure, Joseph Stalin's sweet home Georgia randomly decided to put on the first Soviet rock festival in its fifth-century capital, Tbilisi. Rank-and-file citizens were probably surprised to learn that they did, in fact, have their very own homegrown rock bands:

- Moscow's old-guard *Mashina Vremeni* (**Time Machine**), which celebrated its fiftieth anniversary in 2019. They won a share of the festival's grand prize, and their prog-rock anthem "Crystal City" leads off the official festival album.[1]
- Estonia's jazz-rocky **Magnetic Band**, the other co-winners. Their breakout hit from the festival, "Lady Blues," sounds exactly as fresh and relevant as you would expect of a Soviet song called "Lady Blues."

---

1. The album is called *Spring Rhythms*, and the brave can hear the whole thing on *YouTube*. What a country!

- Leningrad art-rock act **Akvarium**, which showed that as a harbinger of *glasnost*, the festival still left something to be desired. Unlike the other bands, they didn't pre-submit their lyrics for state approval—not that they would have passed muster anyway. Math-degreed leader Boris Grebenshikov was effectively blackballed from Soviet society afterward, thanks to a punk-tinged set that included such shocking themes as marrying your way out of the country.[2]

In case you need refreshing, Georgia is on the southern edge of the Caucasus Mountains between the Black and Caspian seas—geographically Asian, but culturally Extremely Eastern European. As part of the narrow strip of land separating Persia from Russia, and within Hording distance of Mongolia, you can correctly guess that it's been subject to imperial whims for many centuries. But Tbilisi's skyline is still dominated by Narikala, the bluff-set Persian citadel that's been nervously eyeing the Kura River valley for some seventeen hundred years.

Atlanta took on Tbilisi as a sister city in 1988—eight years before Atlanta's own Olympics, and just three years before the Republic of Georgia emerged from the Soviet Union. An associated organization is called the Georgia to Georgia Foundation, underscoring the fact that, yes, their whole relationship is pretty much just based on the fact that they have the same name.[3]

—C.D.S.

2. "Marina told me that she has had enough/That she is all tired and fucked up…/That she is beautiful, but life is in vain/And it is time for her to marry a Finn." Finland didn't bite on the obvious tourism slogan, "Slightly better than death."

3. It's not even really the same name. The US state is named for England's George II, the grandfather of the guy from *Hamilton*; and the republic name most likely comes from *gurgan*, the Persian word for "wolf." Sorry, Southern friends, but that's just objectively a cooler etymology.

Q. In 1991 a replica of the *Santa Maria* was built in what US state capital?

A. Columbus.

In fourteen hundred and ninety-two, Christopher Columbus hit the Americas with three surprisingly janky ships. On Christmas of that fateful year, the ponderous cargo-toting *Santa Maria*[1]—not meant to venture anywhere near land—hit a sandbank along the northern coast of what is now Haiti. This development was anything but *feliz*, but the ship was unceremoniously torn apart and used to build a fort, which Columbus named La Navidad.

Five hundred years later, city officials in Columbus, Ohio, decided to honor their city's namesake with a $1.5 million, life-sized homage to the famous flagship. After floating downtown in the Scioto River for about twenty years, its fate was roughly equal in ignominy to that of the original: crowds stopped visiting, the operating nonprofit folded in 2011, and the thing has been sitting in pieces in a vacant lot since 2013, waiting for someone to pony up millions for restoration or replacement.

The city's still there, though—and now that it isn't a gateway to the fifteenth-century Caribbean, Columbus's main interesting claim to fame is just how *un*-interesting it is. It's long been known as a good place to try out new things, due to its extremely average demographics (*WalletHub* ranked it fourth-most representative) and huge number of college students (2018 enrollment at Ohio State[2] was over 65,000). Accordingly, Columbusites

---

1. The *Santa Maria* is the only one of the three that we call by its official name. Spanish ships of the time were all named for Catholic saints but called by nicknames—hence the *Santa Clara* became *La Niña*, "the little one." *La Pinta* means "the painted one," and it vanished from history so quickly and completely that no one even knows its real name. *¡Que misterioso!*

2. Sorry, Buckeyes: literally no one else cares that it is technically called *The* Ohio State University.

pride themselves on being guinea pigs for horrifying new fast foods; you can thank those kids for garbaging up your sad, sad Friday evenings.[3]

In case you overdose on all that fast food, Columbus has sports too! The NHL's Blue Jackets have been playing, largely unnoticed, since 2000. In Major League Soccer, the Columbus Crew have garnered five more trophies than the Blue Jackets—which is to say, five—and in 2018 narrowly avoided being forcibly moved to Texas, thanks to a local ordinance passed in the wake of the Cleveland Browns' 1990s relocation fiasco.

Oh, and Ohio State has won some stuff too. But never mind that—let's cover some Columbusites in other disciplines!

- **Lil' Bow Wow** gave Ohio a rare rap shout-out in his 2000 debut single, "Bounce With Me." It was so, so def.
- Populist-food hobbit **Guy Fieri** often stops by favorite spots in his hometown, and he has featured a few on *Diners, Drive-Ins and Dives*. Fun fact: Interstates 70 and 71 collectively have zero exits marked "Flavortown."
- More impressive, and (predictably) more obscure: over twenty-nine days in 1964, OSU graduate **Jerrie Mock** became the first woman to fly solo around the world. She was born in Newark, Ohio, some 30 miles east of the capital—but her single-engine Cessna was called the *Spirit of Columbus*.

—N.H.

---

3. Other things to thank Columbus for? Wendy's was founded there, and White Castle is headquartered there. The former gave us the Baconator, and the latter Chicken Rings—which they say are not deep-fried cloacae, but *what other chicken part is shaped like that?*

Q. The first European settlement on Manhattan built its outer defenses on what street?

A. Wall Street.

Well, let's call them "defenses." As we'll soon see, the wall that loomed over Wall Street—de Walstraat in New Amsterdam days—didn't really do much at all.

Despite its great position at the southern tip of Manhattan, Fort Amsterdam was exposed to *land* invaders until they started putting up picket fences along their northern border in the 1640s. In 1652, the First Anglo-Dutch War gave Director General Peter Stuyvesant a more urgent reason to fortify it, so he turned the fences into a bona fide 9-foot wooden wall,[1] with gates, cannon access, and intimidating spikes on top. Then, the war didn't quite make it to Manhattan, so for the time being it was just a 5,000-guilder boondoggle.

A few years later, the Peach Tree War[2] brought hundreds of Susquehannock warriors straight to the foot of the wall…and then around it, as they simply hopped into the Hudson and waded. Recognizing the wall's now-obvious weakness, Stuyvesant had an additional flank built down the western side of the settlement, and raised the whole thing another few feet.[3]

---

1. No Great Wall of China, it stretched just 2,340 feet across the island. That part of Manhattan is about twice as wide now, thanks to landfill (not the smelly kind, just the kind where they, y'know, fill space in with land). On the East River side, the shoreline was extended from Pearl to Water Street, and then Front Street, and *then* they finally stopped their shortsighted naming scheme and called the current one FDR Drive.

2. Begun, according to legend, when a Dutch farmer fatally shot a Native American fruit thief. Basically, America has always been like that.

3. This is also when residents built an earthen tidal barrier at the eastern end. Its name, "Lang de Waal," has caused much confusion regarding Wall Street's origin story. But now you know better!

In 1664 the British finally confronted New Amsterdam for real—and this time the wall did nothing, because they came from the sea. Facing four frigates full of redcoats, Stuyvesant surrendered before a shot was fired, and suddenly the New Amsterdammers were the first New Yorkers.

Mind you, Walstraat was neither the first nor last sketchy wall of note:

- Athens tried to control trade and transportation by building 4-mile **"Long Walls"** from the city to a couple of key ports. Seen as an economic threat, these walls caused friction with Sparta and other rivals, until they were toppled by Roman troops.
- Built in C.E.122, **Hadrian's Wall** was a massive bulwark the Romans built across northern England to keep barbarians out of the empire, and to create an excuse to tax border crossers. It worked fine, but less than twenty years later Antoninus Pius decided it was too far south; he built his own Antonine Wall across the Central Belt of Scotland.
- North Korea's Kim Il-Sung started sounding alarms in 1989, falsely saying the US had helped South Korea build a physical wall across the peninsula on their side of the **demilitarized zone**. He was trying to capitalize on the Berlin-related rise in global anti-wall sentiment; history has not recorded David Hasselhoff's opinion of the controversy.

Back on Manhattan, the new British leadership kept the Waalstraat wall around for a while, but everyone gradually got cranky about its upkeep. In 1699 it was dismantled, and some of its stones (apparently it acquired stones at some point) were recycled into the bastions for a new city hall.

At least they still had bastions!

—L.M.P.

Q. What is the capital of Luxembourg?

A. Luxembourg.

The "World's Most Adorable Country" sash has been artfully tossed over the shoulders of Luxembourg for well over a century. Rightfully so! Its spoken language is Luxembourgish, and its citizens are known as Luxembourgers.[1] Awww! Their main agricultural export is grapes. What an adorable fruit!

In the early 1800s, when the post-Napoleonic Congress of Vienna was burdened with redrawing Western Europe's borders,[2] Luxembourg was allowed to remain a grand duchy—and they're still the world's only one of those. The whole thing is like an Aaron Sorkin treatment for a *Netflix* movie, with Ariana Grande as a pop singer who meet-cutes (meets-cute?) with a dreamy duke.

The national holiday is celebrated on June 23, commemorating the birthday of Grand Duke Henri and, several years ago, the birthday of Grand Duke Jean. Before you start congratulating Luxembourg dukedom on their birthdate synchronicity, you should know that neither was even

---

1. "Luxembourger" is the noun, while the adjective version is just "Luxembourg." This seems both strange and strangely modern: "Luca's reluctance to drive more than 23 kilometers is *so* Luxembourg." See?

2. This has happened pretty frequently throughout history—and despite a complexity that makes *Finnegans Wake* look like setup instructions for an Ikea end table, the Congress of Vienna wasn't an actual congress, and never held any sessions. It was essentially a bunch of likely brandy-fueled chats between the "Great Powers," leading to some superb handshake deals. At least this one turned out better than Iraq!

born in the summer; Luxembourg just uses that date because it's a pleasant time for a national holiday.[3] Adorbs!

Luxembourg's capital is pretty much cobblestones, preserved fortresses, grand plazas, museums, and symphonies—it's a legit, even-more-profitable Epcot. For crying out loud, its flag is a purple lion with a tiny gold crown.

All of this raises the question: just how did a tiny, grape-growing, mostly urban duchy get so rich?

- **Innovation.** Luxembourg halted its coal and iron ore industries decades ago, aiming to become a knowledge economy with a lot of foreign investment. They even have a space agency that's targeting robot exploration of the moon by 2020.
- **Banking.** This is where it gets shady. In 2014 the LuxLeaks scandals revealed Luxembourg as the Caymans of Europe, tax haven–wise. There were a lot of furrowed brows in the EU—but fortunately for Luxembourg, their former prime minister Jean-Claude Juncker had just been elected president of the European Commission. North Korea's Kim family is said to have long kept billions in secret Luxembourg accounts, so…there's that!
- **Media.** Luxembourg embraced commercial radio and TV long before other Euro countries—famously, their broadcasts were where The Beatles first heard Elvis—giving Radio Television Luxembourg a big head start on becoming the largest digital media group in Europe. For all their cultural trappings, RTL is still constantly broadcasting stuff like *The X Factor* and *Pop Idol* to the rest of Europe, loading up on fine wine and pissing across the border into Germany and France. You know, metaphorically speaking.

—J.H.G.

3. See also Presidents' Day in the US, which likewise can never actually fall on the birthday of Washington *or* Lincoln—and should therefore be moved to June as well. "I wish I had another day off in February," said no one.

Q. You'll find the Great Barrier Reef in what sea?

A. Coral Sea.

Stretching from the Australian coast out to the Solomon Islands,[1] the Coral Sea has an Italy-sized swath that's occupied by the Great Barrier Reef, which, unlike the Great Wall of China, you *can* actually see from space.[2] And yup, it's made of coral.

The basic unit of coral is the polyp, basically just a little mouth in a skeleton of calcium carbonate. It's got some primitive guts, tentacles to catch the weensy creatures it noms on, and a sheath of fleshy tissue around its skeleton.

That tissue is where the magic happens. Long ago, corals invited photosynthetic algae called zooxanthellae to live there. In exchange for a well-lit living space and some carbon dioxide, the zooxanthellae provide for nearly all of the coral's metabolic needs, and also supply the bright pigmentation we associate with coral reefs, so they're essentially the backbone of the scuba-industrial complex (even though every creature in this essay is an invertebrate).

They're also the reason why those widespread bleaching events you've heard about are way worse than you thought. Bleaching occurs when seawater gets too warm, and, in an effort to survive, corals chuck out their

1. So named because idiotic Spanish explorer Álvaro de Mendaña de Neira found alluvial gold on Guadalcanal in the 1560s, and so assumed it was *obviously* where biblical King Solomon had hidden his treasure, like a baby-chopping, island-hopping Scrooge McDuck.

2. Furthermore, you can see it *from the moon*. On the *Apollo 15* mission, a reef-spotting inspired crewman Joseph P. Allen to give an apparently impromptu recitation from Captain Cook's *Endeavour* logbook—because, as we must never forget, astronauts kick ass.

zooxanthellae, revealing the white stony skeleton inside the transparent tissue. Bleached corals can and sometimes do bounce back, but it's an uphill battle; without zooxanthellae to provide nutrients, they often just starve to death. And it's a cascade from there: opportunistic algae move in and murk up the water, allowing in less light, which kills more coral, which drives away other ocean life, which disrupts the food chain, which allows predators like the crown-of-thorns starfish[3] to kill more coral. Consulting current climate-change projections, UNESCO estimates that every damn coral in the sea will be dead by 2100.

By the way, this will do much more than mess up your snorkeling holiday. Reefs cover less than 1 percent of the ocean floor, but they're home to more than a quarter of its life. They're the first and last link in the marine food chain, and—this is a big one—they're a huge sink for carbon fixation. In other words, the same atmospheric carbon that traps heat in the ocean and causes bleaching has been partially absorbed in the past by the very corals we're killing.

So how do we stop it? Easy:

- Stop dumping carbon into the atmosphere. Like, yesterday.
- Use reef-safe sunscreen. Oxybenzone is a common sunscreen ingredient, and it kills the crap out of coral.
- Invest in new technologies, such as that starfish-killing underwater robot, which is definitely a real thing and not something we made up. It's called COTSbot (for crown-of-thorns starfish, natch), and it administers lethal injections. Take that, you radially symmetric bastards!

—A.R.

3. Named for Jesus' crown of thorns, which some traditions say came from a jujube bush, which produces a fruit called jujube that inspired both the movie-theater candy and the *RuPaul's Drag Race* contestant of the same name. (She came in third.)

Q. The Canadian postal code H0H 0H0 is reserved for letters to what dude?

A. Santa Claus.

In days of yore, letters to Santa were considered undeliverable and either destroyed or left to gather dust in postal bins. Canada Post—being, well, nice and Canadian—changed that in 1974, rising up in one Santa voice and answering as many as they could. Then in 1982, realizing the golden opportunity presented by their six-character, alternating alphanumeric delivery-zone format, some tragically hip staffer figured out that H0H 0H0 would make a perfect postcode.

The pile of letters kept growing like an arcade fire.[1] In 2017, volunteers put in 260,000 hours to pen 1.6 million replies, each in the language of the original letter (they cite about thirty in any given year, including Braille). Psychologists handle sensitive messages—children begging for a new parent, say, or to be healed from a disease. In 2018, Canada Post workers were on strike for two months before Christmas, but many still volunteered for Santa duty. How Canadian is that?

The Universal Postal Union[2] says that all over the world, letters to Santa, Père Noël, and Father Christmas generate an additional eight million

---

1. Though most come from children, Canadian Santa will answer a request from any Canadians—be they loverboys, men without hats, or even barenaked ladies. It's a rush! (Don't worry, we're done now.)

2. An actual thing, and naturally headquartered in Switzerland. It's now under the auspices of the UN but, having been established in 1874, is more than seventy years older. The UPU is dedicated to helping "ensure a truly universal network of up-to-date products and services"; if nothing else, we can attest that it's up-to-date in say-nothing corporate speak.

pieces of mail each year. And Canada's not the only country with a special program to handle them:

- In **Finland** the elf staff fields 500,000-plus letters at the branch in Rovaniemi, a town of sixty thousand, within a snowball's throw of the Arctic Circle.
- In the **US**, parents have to include their own Santa reply and a self-addressed stamped envelope. A crew in Anchorage, Alaska, is the keeper of the special North Pole postmark—complete with the 99705 ZIP Code of the *actual* town called North Pole, near Fairbanks (but still some 1,700 miles from the actual *actual* North Pole).
- In the **UK**, the Royal Mail handles 800,000 letters to Father Christmas at Santa's Grotto in Reindeerland ("unfortunately," their website says, "we are unable to give a precise location on the map for this postcode"). The Brits also accept donations with the letters, to fund programs that aid child-abuse survivors—so who cares how close it is to anything?

Meanwhile, back in Canada, not even Santa is immune to a petty geopolitical beef. He became a player in the 2013 debate with Russia over sovereignty of the North Pole,[3] with future prime minister Justin Trudeau saying, "Everyone knows that Santa Claus is Canadian. His postal code is H0H 0H0."

If we'd paid five cents for that argument, we would want our nickel back. (Sorry!)

—L.C.

---

3. For the record, international law governs the high seas, including the Arctic Sea. Technically, the North Pole is sovereign territory unto itself, like the Vatican. Which brings up a whole other age-old Christmas dispute…

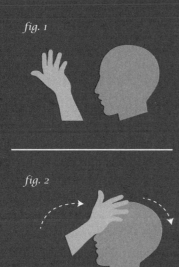

fig. 1

fig. 2

fig. 3

7

UH-OH, IT'S A SCIENCE CHAPTER

Q. What is the only planet in our solar system not named for a deity?

A. Earth.

There are upward of 800,000 identified objects in the solar system: one star, five dwarf planets, eight major planets, 185 moons (of major planets), more than six thousand comets, and a whole mess of asteroids. They are named for gods, goddesses, heroes, and villains. But our planet? Cradle of mankind? We went with dirt.

Earth. Terra. Tierra. Erde. Dìqiú. Prithvī. Maapallo. A rose by any other name might smell as sweet, but our name comes from the ground beneath our feet. It's pretty lame; consider, for instance, that it took until 1978 for some random asteroid to be named for Hephaestus, the Greek god of metallurgy and volcanoes. Even now, there's no (real) celestial body named for his Roman equivalent, Vulcan.[1] We could still name ourselves for a god of volcanoes, dude!

But whatever. "Earth" comes from Old English, *eorthe*, and Germanic, *erde*—and yeah, they both mean "dirt," which is pretty self-explanatory. Maybe it's a generational thing: when people spent most of their time dodging wolves and dying from dysentery, coming up with clever names for the rock we all live on was probably a pretty low priority.

---

1. Vulcan *was* the name of a proposed planet, believed for a time to orbit between Mercury and the sun. In 1859, French mathematician Urbain Le Verrier found minor irregularities in Mercury's orbit and suggested a small planet might cause the observed motion (he wasn't just spitballing—he'd used the same technique to predict the location of Neptune). Several astronomers claimed to have observed the hypothetical planet, but the orbital irregularities were finally explained in 1916 by a little ditty you've probably heard of: Einstein's theory of general relativity.

At least we can look to the sky and ponder the cool names for some other solar system stuff:

- Astronomers' original nickname for the dwarf planet **Makemake**, which hangs out in the Kuiper Belt with poor old Pluto, was "Easterbunny." God forbid anyone should have any fun in space, though, so instead they chose to name it for the Rapa Nui fertility god—the Rapa Nui live on…wait for it…Easter Island. Oh, you wag astronomers!

- The **Oort Cloud**, which sounds like one of those weird apocalyptic villains from the original *Star Trek*,[2] but is really just named for a twentieth-century Dutch astronomer. The cloud forms a really, really big sphere around the sun,[3] filled with about a trillion comets and other icy space junk; you could consider it the Slushy of the Gods.

- **Centaurs.** Yep, that's right: they're half-man, half-horse, and they're all over the outer solar system. None of that is true, but the reality is sooo booooring. "Centaurs" are a class of things between Jupiter and Neptune that behave sort of like asteroids and sort of like comets. That is *massively* less interesting than some ancient Greek dude who was so hard up that he got it on with a horse.

—A.W.

---

2. See also: the killer cornucopia, the killer amoeba, the killer space web, the killer glowy sphere. They had kind of a theme going.

3. I mean, *really* big. Like, to get out of it, you'd have to go 100,000 times the distance from the sun to the Earth. Even if you were traveling at the speed of light, that would take a year and a half. Plus, then you'd be stuck in interstellar space, so you should probably think that through.

Q. How many astronauts flew on each of the manned Gemini missions?

A. Two.

In 1962, you may recall, President Kennedy made the audacious call that the US would put a man on the moon by the end of the decade. Mind you, they had just figured out how to get a man into *Earth* orbit months earlier. The longest US spaceflight to date was under 5 hours, and it only reached a distance of 167 miles from Earth; a moon mission would take more than a *week*, and would head out some 240,000 miles.

NASA had a lot to learn before it could achieve all that. Enter Project Gemini,[1] named for its pairs of astronaut "twins."

One of the more mundane necessities was to figure out how to feed astronauts. John Glenn had chugged a tube of applesauce during Project Mercury, but more options were needed for longer missions.[2] One such (unofficial) option was ruled out by John W. Young on *Gemini 3*: 2 hours after takeoff, he surprised crewmate Gus Grissom with a corned beef sandwich he had stashed away in his pocket. Gus took a bite, but crumbs started flying everywhere—potentially deadly crumbs that could float into electrical instruments and cause them to fail. Luckily, no damage was done, but Congress was not amused, and Young got a formal reprimand. As for Grissom, his memorial museum now displays a replica of the

---

1. The dictionary says it's "JEM-uh-nye," like you probably say it, but NASA's official pronunciation was "Jiminy," like everyone's favorite cricket. I guess they were *kinda* wishing upon a star?

2. In 1964, NASA held a Conference on Nutrition in Space and Related Waste Problems. One pull quote from the conference: "The most practical solution to the waste-disposal problem has been a constipated astronaut."

sandwich—so basically, a fake deli sandwich is one of the most interesting things in Indiana.

Future missions saw fewer hijinks and more achievements:

- On *Gemini 4*, Ed White became the first American to perform a spacewalk. White remarked, "I feel like a million dollars"—in fact a gross understatement, since the mission cost about $100 million.
- *Gemini 5* broke the Soviets' record for longest manned space mission. Its ominous slogan was "8 Days or Bust," but the mission wrapped after seven days, 22 hours, and 55 minutes. Close enough, right?
- *Gemini 7*, which oddly was launched a few days before *Gemini 6* (because of an aborted launch), set a space endurance record of thirteen days and almost 19 hours. The mission, which also saw the first manned space rendezvous, was even longer than the eight-day journey of *Apollo 11*. One giant-*er* leap!

Neil Armstrong's first—and second-to-last—time in space was on *Gemini 8*. The mission saw two spacecraft docked in orbit for the first time, an important step toward a future moon mission. After the docking, though, things went awry. A short circuit caused a thruster to start firing erratically, making the craft spin almost a full revolution per second and blurring the astronauts' vision. Armstrong was somehow still able to think, and he came up with a solution to stop the tumbling, using the reentry thrusters.

That quick thinking must have impressed the right people, because three years later Armstrong was given the honor of commanding the first moon mission—leading to the later, greater honor of being portrayed by Ryan Gosling.[3]

—M.S.

3. In *First Man*, a 2018 film that *The New York Times* called "strangely underwhelming."

Q. *Stinktier* is the German word for what mammal?

A. Skunk.

Tier, by the way, just means "animal," so "stink-animal." Germans never met a compound word they didn't like, and they hardly dropped that habit when they got to the animal kingdom:

- *Tintenfisch*, literally "ink fish," is a squid. It would also be a pretty good name for an office-supplies app.
- *Fledermaus*, or "flutter mouse," is a bat.[1] It would also be a pretty good name for a toddler thrash-metal band.
- *Nacktschnecke*, or "naked snail," is a slug. It would not be a good name for anything else—just try saying *nacktschnecke* out loud. But first, put on a poncho.

In fact, the Teutonic habit of stringing together an entire sentence's worth of letters into one long word is so famous that Mark Twain snarked about it in his 1880 essay, "The Awful German Language." Citing words like *Freundschaftsbezeigungen* ("tokens of friendship") and *Stadtverordneten-versammlungen* ("city council assembly"), Twain correctly said that "these things are not words, they are alphabetical processions."

---

1. And an operetta by Austrian composer Johann Strauss Jr. (better known for "The Blue Danube," a.k.a. the waltz you think of, if any, when you think of the word *waltz*). There are no actual bats in *Die Fledermaus*, just a dude who dresses up as one at a costume ball. The hero Vienna needed?

But back to skunks, German and otherwise: their weapons-grade smell come from glands in the anus called apocrine glands.[2] And of course we do mean "weapons-grade" literally—the *stinktier* uses its *stink* to keep predators at bay. But it would really rather not: a skunk has only about enough musk in its glands for five or six sprays, and reloading can take up to ten days. So if you scare a skunk, it'll probably let you know first by non-olfactory means such as stomping the ground, fluffing its tail, or making semi-adorable pissed-off skunk noises. This is basic woodland diplomacy; it's hoping you'll run away without needing to spray you.

Skunks' reputation as stinky little varmints doesn't stop people from owning them as pets—surgically de-scented, of course. It's illegal in thirty-six states, and you need a permit in most of the others. But should you be one of the intrepid few who chooses a skunk over a cat or cockatiel, you can meet up with like-minded individuals and their stripy, stinky companions at Skunk Fest, an annual festival that's been going on in the suburbs of Cleveland since 2001.[3]

If you're more like the majority who *don't* want a skunk on their property, you should do obvious things like covering your garbage cans, and less obvious things like not overwatering your lawn, because skunks' favorite foods include garbage and grubs. If it's too late, and you've already got a skunk living in a hole around your house, you may be able to entice it away with smelly cheese, another skunk delicacy.

Say what you will about 'em, but they're dedicated to the bit.

—S.D.Z.

---

2. You have apocrine glands in the same general part of your body—and on your eyelids. We don't recommend trying to smell either set.

3. "Bring your family to the most exciting event of the year!" shouted its 2018 flyer, even though the main attractions included seeing different-colored skunks and (seriously) a skunk beauty contest. But it's not all carefree fun: "Do NOT let the public touch your skunk," the flyer mysteriously warned.

Q. Naphthenic acid and palmitic acid were the original ingredients of what substance?

A. Napalm.

Napalm's two namesakes are rough customers even by themselves. Naphthenic acids are among the nastiest pollutants in the wastewater glorped out by oil refineries, and palmitic acid makes up much of the saturated fats found in meat, dairy, and palm oil (duh),[1] and has been tagged by the WHO as a major risk factor for heart disease.

This unsavory couple had their meet-cute on Valentine's Day 1942, in a secret World War II research lab at Harvard. Before then, some primitive napalm-like substances (usually gasoline thickened with rubber) had been used in flamethrowers, but the resultant gouts tended to mostly burn off in the air, the remainder sliding too quickly off their targets to create a proper hellscape. Harvard chemistry professor Louis Fieser solved this problem by combining the aluminum salts of our star-crossed acids (along with a pinch of old-fashioned sawdust) to create a viscous brown jelly that would cling to the unfortunate buildings and/or humans while the burning fuel did its work. The military was intrigued, and a series of tests began, including:

- A preliminary run conducted by Fieser on Harvard's waterlogged soccer field, to the surprise of some nearby tennis players. Since that fireball went up on the Fourth of July, we hereby declare this the most American thing ever.

1. By the way, the razing of rainforests by Indonesia's booming palm oil industry is rapidly killing off the orangutan and Sumatran rhino. Palm oil is in about half of all packaged supermarket products, so enjoy your cookies with a nice tall glass of guilt.

- Early field tests in which the US Army's Chemical Warfare Service (yeah, we totally had one of those) hired German- and Japanese-born architects to create model enemy villages…complete with realistic children's toys. Points for honesty, I guess?
- Project X-Ray, which tested the viability of using hibernating bats, awakened and scattered by a sudden rush of heat, to deliver incendiary bombs.[2] Results were, uh, mixed. One batch of bats was accidentally frozen to death instead of being put into hibernation. Another woke up too fast, escaped their handlers, and burned down a brand-new base near the testing grounds. Quoth the laconic Fieser: "We made a little mistake out there."

Once the kinks were worked out, millions of gallons of napalm were deployed in both theaters of World War II: blasted out by tanks, fired by the suddenly fashionable flamethrower, or dropped via (non-bat-guided) bombs.

While the chemical makeup has changed—modern "napalm" contains neither of its namesakes—burning gel has been a staple of pretty much every major conflict since. Its notoriety peaked with its indiscriminate use in Vietnam,[3] and a 1980 UN protocol banned its use on "concentrations of civilians."

The US waited until 2009 to sign said protocol, tacking on a proviso that it would disregard the treaty whenever doing so would "cause fewer casualties." I love the smell of irony in the morning!

—E.K.

2. X-Ray was the brainchild of Lytle Adams, a Pennsylvania dentist who called the bat "the lowest form of life…associated in history with the underworld and regions of darkness and evil." Writing in support of Adams's proposals, FDR insisted, "This man is not a nut," which, if you find yourself having to say that…

3. Kim Phúc, shown fleeing her village in the famous "Napalm Girl" photo, now runs a foundation that aids young war victims. Go give her your money, like, now: she's at KimFoundation.com.

Q. What ninety-second element was discovered in the same decade as the seventh planet from the sun?

A. Uranium.

Fans of *Fallout 4* will have heard the song "Uranium Fever," originally recorded following the nuclear power rush of the 1940s and 1950s.[1] But way earlier, in the 1780s, William Herschel discovered the first planet that's invisible to the naked eye, setting off Uranus Fever.

Because the 1700s are full of people like this, Herschel wasn't even a trained astronomer. The organist at England's Octagon Chapel in Bath, he was initially impressed by a work on musical harmonics by philosopher Robert Smith.[2] And so he moved on to Smith's book about optics, eventually leading him to build his own telescopes.

Meanwhile, Herschel shared his German heritage (and interest in misunderstanding faraway things) with King George III, who was then busy losing the American Revolution. On March 13, 1781, when Herschel saw what he first thought was a comet—then a star, then a planet[3]—he wanted

---

1. The title of the song, by Arkansas country star Elton Britt, did not refer to lung cancer, black lung, tuberculosis, or emphysema, even though uranium miners faced a heightened risk of all those diseases, according to a later mortality study by the National Institute for Occupational Safety and Health.

2. Not the guy from The Cure, although his musical works also frequently inspire people to look in dark places.

3. Like most early astronomers, Herschel was wrong a lot. As he said in a then-unpublished note of 1778, "I am almost convinced that those numberless small circuses we see on the moon are the works of the Lunarians and may be called their towns." We now know them as craters, and most everyone mentioned in this essay has one named for him. Not poor King George, though.

to name it for the king, a decision his fellow astronomers in *non*-British countries gave some understandable side-eye.

Enter Hamburg astronomer Johann Elert Bode, who figured that since Saturn was Jupiter's father, the next planet should be named for Saturn's dad. Why nobody noticed that Uranus is a Greek name—the only one we use for a planet!—is one of science's least important mysteries.

Bode was friends with Martin Heinrich Klaproth, a chemist who later discovered an element in the yellow-ceramic mineral pitchblende. He named it uranium, in honor of his buddy and "as a kind of memorial" to the planet's discovery in the same decade. That sorted, Klaproth went on to name titanium after the titans, and the decidedly less-catchy tellurium, from the Latin for "earth." There were places where "uranium" was a thing before "Uranus," by the way: at least one British almanac was still trying to make Planet Georgium happen until 1850.

Because scientists are often fantasy nerds, there are a bunch of other elements named for mythic characters, including:

- **Niobium**, found in 1801 and named for Niobe, the daughter of king Tantalus, who has a different element named for him (tantalum, duh). Americans hung on to the name "columbium" until the 1950s, because...Americans.
- **Cerium**, independently discovered in 1803 by Klaproth and Swedes Wilhelm Hisinger and Jöns Jacob Berzelius, and named for the recently discovered asteroid, which in turn is named for the Roman goddess of Froot Loops. Sorry, agriculture *including* cereal grains, of which we assume there must be some in Froot Loops.
- **Thorium**, for the Norse god of thunder. Berzelius, who discovered it in 1828, was Swedish, and probably sick of all the Greco-Roman names. Thorium oxide is heat-resistant and good against the fire giants—plus Chris Hemsworth would look great in it.

—S.B.

Q. The great ape family consists of chimpanzees, gorillas, orangutans, and what other genus?

A. Humans.

It's true: genus *Homo* belongs to the family Hominidae, which in addition to the living great apes, includes extinct ancestors of all us living apes, an evolutionary lineage that goes back some eighteen million years. And shit got a little weird back in the day. Check it:

- *Gigantopithecus blacki* was a towering 10-foot-tall relative of modern orangutans,[1] which probably lived contemporaneously with *Homo erectus* in Southeast Asia. A lumbering, ground-dwelling herbivore, it looked exactly like Bigfoot (the cryptid, not the monster truck).
- *Paranthropus boisei*, an African hominid, is often called the Nutcracker Man for its gigantic teeth, four times the size of ours. *P. boisei* appeared five million years after the split between the human and ape lines, but evolved in a pretty ape-y direction; while it walked upright and maybe used tools, its jaws and dentition have way more in common with gorillas than people. We'll bet it liked to fling poop too.
- *Homo floresiensis* was a tiny little fella on one Indonesian island, discovered in 2003, that happens to be the only hominid that

---

1. In comparison, big-screen Hulk is a puny 8 feet tall and weighs 1,400 pounds (to Dr. Bruce Banner's 128). We know that matter cannot be created or destroyed, so our old pal Einstein's energy-mass equivalence formula (via some dedicated comic-forum geeks) tells us that 45 trillion megajoules of gamma radiation would be required for him to gain that extra mass each time he hulks out. That works out to 12,500 terawatt-hours, or about seven thousand times the Earth's annual energy budget. HULK SMASH PHYSICS!

(indirectly) got a cease-and-desist order from the Tolkien estate. Because scientists are nerds, they nicknamed the 3-foot specimen "the hobbit." After getting J.R.R. shade from beyond the grave, they dutifully changed it to "the halfling" (not really—and that's *probably* the last Dungeons & Dragons joke in this book).

Despite what creationists say,[2] there really are no "missing links" in the fossil record. Science has a pretty good picture of how humans and modern apes evolved—from *Nakalipithecus*, a late common ancestor of humans, chimps, and gorillas; to *Ardipithecus*, possibly the first species after the human line diverged from *Panina*;[3] to the dozens of hominids scattered across the Old World.

It isn't as cut-and-dried as previously assumed, though. There are all sorts of tangles and snarls and dead ends, and as we find more fossils, the timeline of anatomically modern humans keeps getting revised. A 2017 find in Morocco, for instance, shoved things back by a third; we now know *H. sapiens* is at least 300,000 years old.

This, of course, is to say nothing of your mom. *She's* so old, Charles Darwin's phone contacts just have her listed as "O.G." *Snap!*

—A.R.

2. They say a lot! For instance, Answers in Genesis—run by Bill Nye–debater and Ahab cosplayer Ken Ham—posits that *H. erectus* fossils were probably just refugees from the Tower of Babel. For those keeping score at home, the Tower of Babel was allegedly built around 2200 B.C.E., while the oldest *H. erectus* fossil dates to 1.8 million years ago. Also, upright or no, *H. erectus* weren't quite people. But nice try!

3. "Panina" means the chimpanzee genus *Pan*, but it sounds delicious. Incidentally, genus *Pan* comes from the horny Greek trickster god, whereas *panini* comes from the Latin for "bread." And *Pan* the 2015 movie comes from Hugh Jackman wanting a bigger house.

Q. Astronauts Gene Cernan and John W. Young died in what city?

A. Houston.

As commander of *Apollo 17*, Gene Cernan was the eleventh (and last, so far) person to walk on the moon. John W. Young had the longest career of any American astronaut, and flew everything from the *Apollo* modules to the *Space Shuttle*. They are two of only three people who traveled to the moon twice,[1] and after that they both worked for and/or consulted for NASA for several more decades before dying in 2017 and 2018, respectively. And they did it all in Houston, the home of NASA's Johnson Space Center.

The original Mission Control Center was a real Tomorrowland marvel back in its day. We're talking miles of pneumatic tubes, thousands of miles of wires, and hundreds of horn-rimmed, chain-smoking men in shirt-sleeves. Built from 1961, shortly after John F. Kennedy called for a moon shot timeline of eight and a half years, it wound up in Southeast Texas because Houston met NASA's stringent site-selection guidelines, including (seriously) ice-free waters for barge transport.[2] Since then, what is now Johnson Space Center has been the center for planning and after-launch mission support of all crewed US spaceflights.

---

1. Jim Lovell is the other, and, as the commander of *Apollo 13*, he's also the only one who went there twice without actually setting foot on it. He did get to meet Tom Hanks, though, so that's something.

2. It also had the endorsement of homeboy and then–vice president Lyndon B. Johnson, for whom it was named after he died in 1973. He also said, at his 1965 inauguration, "We are all fellow passengers on a dot of earth." He wasn't even high!

But to make space exploration more of a nationwide effort, NASA spread other facilities from sea to shining sea:

- Found in the Maryland-side DC suburbs, the **Goddard Space Flight Center** is the oldest NASA site and oversees stuff like the Hubble and upcoming James Webb Space Telescope. It's named for rocketry pioneer Robert H. Goddard, who once said, "The dream of yesterday is the hope of today and the reality of tomorrow."
- Pasadena, California, is home to the **Jet Propulsion Laboratory**, which sends probes out to the solar system and beyond. Early in its NASA career, JPL designed the unmanned mission that preceded *Apollo* to the moon, and they've been probing the surface of Mars since the mid-seventies. But maybe the most famous JPL project is *Voyager 1*, which launched in 1977 and is, as of this writing, still communicating from about 13.5 *billion* miles away.
- Not *quite* the same thing as Cape Canaveral, **Kennedy Space Center** is on Merritt Island, Florida. Part of the reason why they launch rockets from there is the Earth's rotation: it's faster closer to the equator, to the tune of about 914 mph at that particular spot on the Atlantic coast. Launching the rockets eastward gives them a nice velocity boost, which saves all-important rocket fuel.[3]

Back in Houston, the original Mission Control ceased operations in 1992—now it's elsewhere within the same complex. But the room just got a thorough $5 million sprucing up for the fiftieth anniversary of the *Apollo 11* moon landing, returning it to authentic sixties condition, ashtrays and all. Well, not *all*. The smoke itself won't be there—they banned it in 1991.

—T.C.

3. For the same reason, the European Space Agency launches from faraway French Guiana, at a latitude of a mere 5 degrees. The Russians, on the other hand, couldn't get any farther south than Baikonur, Kazakhstan; at nearly 46 degrees, it's farther north than Minneapolis and Montréal.

Q. How many carbon atoms are there in a molecule of octane?

A. Eight.

At the dawn of the twentieth century, there were *three* competing automotive fuels. Steam had the longest pedigree, but in the cold it could take 45 minutes to get the damned engine boiling. Electric cars were popular mainly with city dwellers, as the scarcity of good roads meant you couldn't really leave town anyway (then as now, battery range was the main limiting factor).

And then there was the internal combustion engine. Noisy, stinky, and with manual gears and hand-cranked starters that turned every grocery run into a workout, gasoline technology had its drawbacks. But after Henry Ford graced a bevy of new highways with his cheap and cheerful Model T—soon to feature Charles Kettering's electric starter—the fates of the other engines were sealed.

One problem: to keep gasoline from igniting before it gets sparked—making a telltale, engine-busting "knock"—you need anti-knock additives (duh). The main one was tetraethyl lead (TEL), from the early 1920s all the way up until the seventies, when people finally started caring that it's way poisonous.[1] Since then we've been using "unleaded" gasoline—nowadays, mostly ethanol (the same kind of alcohol you drink), and an aromatic

1. Thomas Midgley Jr. the discoverer of TEL's anti-knock properties, once had to take several months' leave thanks to lead poisoning. "Can you imagine how much money we're going to make with this?" he nonetheless asked his boss (Charles Kettering, of electric-starter fame). Midgley later championed refrigeration by chlorofluorocarbons (CFCs), nigh-singlehandedly ripping open the ozone layer. One of his inventions killed him too: having lost the use of his legs to polio in 1940, he was strangled by the hoist he used to get in and out of bed.

refining by-product called BTEX (which you should very much not). All these things raise the fuel's "octane rating."[2]

Because higher ratings mean better-performing engines, the phrase "high octane" has come to stand for anything that's powerful or generally kick-ass. Hence:

- Octane was a Decepticon who changed into a plane and an oil truck in the original Transformers universe. Also known as Tankor, his page at TFWiki.net calls him "a cheat, a liar, and a coward who thinks only of himself and can't be trusted any further than Megatron can throw Devastator."[3]
- *Octane* is a 2005 album by prog-rock band Spock's Beard. In the fast 2-minute instrumental section that opens it, you'll hear some of the best theremin work this side of your stoner uncle's basement.
- In auto-themed Lego sets, Octan has long been a fictional gas brand. But in 2014's *The Lego Movie* it diversified, doing everything from construction, to the top-rated TV show *Where Are My Pants?*, to apparently all the world's voting machines—all under the direction of the evil Will Ferrell.

As of this writing, the electric car is still climbing in its comeback, with the Tesla Model 3 having passed the old-guard Ford Fusion and Nissan Sentra on the sales charts in a recent quarter. Of course, it still can't go more than, like, 200 miles past them.

—C.D.S.

2. Mind you, they have nothing to do with actual octane. Crude-oil refining produces straight-chain hydrocarbon molecules of varying lengths—hexane has six carbon atoms; octane, eight. Autoigniting at low pressures, they all suck as fuel. But with three of its carbons branched off the chain, an isomer called *iso*octane has the highest ignition point of them all, and is thus the 100-point paragon on which the "octane rating" is based.

3. That distance is frustratingly unspecified.

Q. An aqueous solution always contains what inorganic compound?

A. Water.

Water is often called the universal solvent, because so many other chemicals dissolve in its liquid embrace. For exactly one example, water + sodium + chloride = saltwater.[1]

H_2O is an extremely effective solvent because the hydrogen side of the molecule has a positive charge and the oxygen side is negative, allowing water molecules to attract ions of other molecules. In the case of table salt, this breaks up the crystalline structure and turns it into a solution.

There is a saying among people who try too hard that "dilution is the solution to pollution."[2] It's true, but it only works for water-soluble stuff; hydrophobic chemicals are a real headache to deal with, since they will often build up in the fatty tissue of fish and animals instead of hanging out in the water column, diluting contaminants and such. That's how you get nightmare pollution like polychlorinated biphenyls (PCBs), the carcinogenic coolants that in some areas are considered a threat to human health and the environment at a few parts per quadrillion (that's fifteen zeros, homes). This would not be a problem if, like the lakes on Saturn's moon Titan, our oceans were filled with liquid methane. That would

---

1. If you combine water and neutral sodium, you get a big frickin' explosion. If you combine water and diatomic chlorine—a deadly gas—you get a frickin' swimming pool. Chemistry is weird!

2. Who says something similar? Homeopaths! Supporters of that pseudoscience follow the law of minimum dose—essentially, that the lower the concentration of a purported active ingredient, the *more* powerful the mixture is supposed to be. By this logic, if you drink distilled water, you will become more powerful than Darth Vader can possibly imagine.

dilute the crap out of those PCBs—but would, uh, probably create other problems.

So, water is the universal solvent. Does that mean it's the right solvent for you? If you still have any doubts, consider these alternative solvents:

- **Water** is a polar solvent, great for dissolving salt and blood and polar bears (not really). Ethanol, the alcohol in all our drinks, goes that one better by having both polar *and* non-polar properties, which is why it mixes with gasoline. Oh alcohol, there truly is no problem you cannot cure!
- **Methylene chloride** is a solvent often used to strip bathtubs for refinishing. Because the fumes are heavier than air, they tend to build up inside the tubs, and there have been occasions where the refinisher has inhaled too much and died, leading to an embarrassing conversation at the pearly gates.
- A popular dry-cleaning solvent, **perchloroethylene** can get a burger stain out of a shirt with ease—and can also seep right through a concrete floor and enter the groundwater.[3] The solvent becomes the solute, which would be funnier if it weren't so devastating.

—A.W.

---

3. A dry-cleaning chemical that's more environmentally friendly? Supercritical carbon dioxide! Yes, the global-warming supervillain can greenly spiff up your interview suit—which is no weirder than seasoning your fries with differently charged versions of an explosive metal and an actual chemical warfare agent. Seriously, chemistry!

Q. In quantum physics, what word refers to any particle that follows Bose–Einstein statistics?

Yes, now a liberal arts major will attempt to tackle particle physics. Hoo boy. Okay.

Broad strokes, all atoms are made up of two types of particles: fermions[1] and bosons. Fermions are protons, neutrons, electrons, and a half dozen other things. Bosons include photons, that vaunted Higgs particle, and the hypothetical graviton. So, what makes a boson different?

All you really need to know is that fermions are matter particles—they comprise, you know, *stuff*—whereas bosons are field quanta: little packets of force that tell that stuff how to interact.[2] Photons, for instance, relay electromagnetic force, while others called W and Z bosons mediate weak nuclear force. The reason why it was such a big deal to finally find the Higgs boson a few years back is because it's the one that gives mass to other particles. *Heavy*.

Anyway, the things are named for one Satyendra Nath Bose, the smartest dude you've never heard of. Born in Kolkata in 1894, he had a master's degree by age twenty-one, and translated Einstein's relativity papers into English at twenty-five (from German—he spoke seven languages in all).

---

1. Named for Enrico Fermi, Manhattan Project member and architect of the atomic bomb. He also holds a 1940 US patent for a "Process for the production of radioactive substances." For some reason, we can't find the abstract online.

2. And this is of course far, far more complicated than we go into here, since groups of fermions can somehow also be bosons, as can atomic nuclei themselves. Helium is a boson: if you get it really, really cold, it becomes a superfluid and does crazy-ass things like climb out of an open vessel by itself, and then presumably becomes self-aware.

He then basically invented the field of quantum statistics, in order to prove Planck's quantum radiation law. Albert Einstein lobbied on his behalf to have that paper published, and the pair went off to Paris to produce research that would predict the existence of bosons—work Peter W. Higgs and François Englert would later build on to win their 2013 Nobel.[3]

Later, Bose took a teaching post in Dhaka, Bangladesh, and continued to publish papers on X-ray crystallography, statistics, number theory, magnetism, and a unified field theory. As if that weren't enough, he also dabbled in physiology, mineralogy, and zoology. *And* he still found time to:

- Tutor his university friend—Dhurjati Prasad Mukerji, the father of Indian sociology—through a bout of temporary blindness while Mukerji studied for an Egyptian-history degree. Young Bose was a mere history dilettante, but when Mukerji told the professor that Bose had helped him crush the exam, the professor reportedly said, "That explains it."
- Pen a deliciously salty letter about the denial of his US visa application: "Your Senator [Joseph] McCarthy objected to the fact that I had seen Russia first."
- Write poetry and play a bowed string instrument, the *esraj*. Apparently he was pretty good at both.

Meanwhile, we're over here struggling with a joke about how "Bose" sounds like "bows." Huh-huh.

—A.R.

---

3. Bose was nominated four times but never won a Nobel. Of the 209 Nobel laureates in physics, only two of them were from India. In fact, just sixteen weren't from Europe, Australia, or the Americas. Meanwhile, in 2018, the list got its *third woman ever*. Seriously, dudes.

Q. Leghorn is a breed of what animal?

A. Chicken.

It's going to take some work to get from an Italian city that isn't even called Leghorn, to a cartoon rooster that doesn't even *look* like a Leghorn, so let's get to it.

In the 1500s the British navy showed up in the Tuscan port city of Livorno. Thus began a centuries-long symbiotic relationship—they established a presence in the Mediterranean for king and country,[1] while providing local security for the ruling Medici family. To this very day, the Brits, who can always be relied upon to bastardize foreign names of any kind, sometimes call the city "Leghorn."

Fast-forward to the 1850s, and a Connecticuter known to history only as Captain Gates noticed that North Italy was home to a small, industrious, light-eating chicken.[2] Instantly realizing the profit potential, he brought the breed home, and by the 1870s Leghorn chickens were among America's most popular.

Jumping again to 1945, the Warner Bros. Animation studio was working on the second *Merrie Melodies* cartoon to star confused, combative chicken-hunter Henery Hawk. The short would introduce a foil for Henery,

1. Livorno is still home to Italy's oldest British cemetery. Its eternal residents include that magnificent Tory maverick John Pollexfen Bastard (1756–1816).

2. The domesticated chicken is a relatively recent innovation. It didn't catch on until Egyptians unlocked the secrets of incubation, thereby getting tasty eggs (which came first, at least as a food) around 700 B.C.E. That may sound like a long time ago, but goats, sheep, and cattle were all tamed some seven millennia earlier. By 700 B.C.E., the Pyramids of Giza were nearly 1,800 years old—no spring chickens!

a giant unnamed rooster with a blustery Southern-trickster persona, based on a local-to-L.A. 1930s radio character named The Sheriff.[3]

About that same time, though, NBC radio's *The Fred Allen Show* debuted another Southern blowhard named Senator Claghorn. His pronounced Dixie drawl was so broad and hilarious that water coolers and malt shops across America were soon crowded with people yelling, "That's a joke, son."

The frenemy chemistry between the Warners' hawk and rooster was apparently a hit as well. In 1948 they made their third appearance together (of an eventual eleven), with the chicken's voice sounding more and more like Fred Allen's cornpone kahuna. The short was called *The Foghorn Leghorn*—and you've got to admit, "Leghorn" sounds more like "Claghorn" than it does "Livorno."

It's easier to trace some of the other Warner cartoons' names:

- **Bugs Bunny** is named for director Ben "Bugs" Hardaway. Later demoted by the more-legendary Friz Freleng in a standard case of office politics, Hardaway peaced out to Walter Lantz Productions, where he developed, and spent five years as the voice of, Woody Woodpecker. (We're not even sorry for putting that voice in your head right now.)
- **Sylvester J. Pussycat** isn't named for any particular Sylvester (there aren't many to choose from, and he debuted before Stallone was even born), but for the European wildcat, *Felis silvestris*, which in turn comes from the Latin for "woodland"—or as he'd say, "foretht."
- **Porky Pig** is made of pork. Just sit with that thought for a moment.

—C.D.S.

---

3. And a coloration—pure white body, with a dark brown head and tail—that apparently isn't found in real-life roosters at all. Of course, it's also not common to find roosters who stand 5-feet, 2-inches. Or, you know, talk.

fig. 1

fig. 2

fig. 3

8

IT'S LIT

207

Q. Moby-Dick belonged to what species of whale?

A. Sperm whale.[1]

Though it's long been synonymous with bottomless allegorical soul-searching, when Herman Melville wrote *Moby-Dick* in 1851, the novel was practically ripped from the headlines. Melville's magnum opus was based in no small measure on the real-world adventures of the albino sperm whale called Mocha Dick, which roamed the seas near Chile between 1810 and 1838. Named for a local island—and, um, dick[2]—Mocha was reported to have swum peacefully alongside whaling vessels until disturbed, whereupon he lashed out violently against the whaleboats sent after him.

Unlike his fictional kinswhale, Mocha Dick apparently ended his suzerainty of the seas at the end of a whaler's lance, though intermittent sightings of other white whales gave him an Elvis-like afterlife[3] for decades thereafter.

---

1. a.k.a. *Physeter macrocephalus*, "blowhole big-head." If you said "white whale," too bad: taxonomically, that term refers to the family *Monodontidae*, comprising the narwhal and the beluga whale, which are not particularly close relatives of Moby's. You can totally tell, too—despite their unicorn tusks, which can top 8 feet in length, wild narwhals are known to have terrorized neither whaleships nor attention-deficient sophomores.

2. Sort of. "Dick" was meant as an anonymous sobriquet, like John Doe—a usage that's lived on in the generic expression "Tom, Dick, or Harry." That's not to say that Melville was a stranger to penetrative prose, intentional or otherwise: while taking a break from *Moby*, he once wrote that Nathaniel Hawthorne "shoots his strong New England roots into the hot soil of my Southern soul." Damn, son.

3. The King himself was apparently a fan of the 1956 film adaptation of *Moby-Dick*, the one with Gregory Peck. In his famous comeback special twelve years later, Presley picked up a microphone stand and mimicked harpooning a whale, shouting "Moby Dick!," before launching into "Don't Be Cruel." Dude was weird, you know?

The other real-world inspiration for Melville's revenge epic was the *Essex*, a whaling vessel sunk by a massive sperm whale in 1820 in the South Pacific, leaving the survivors adrift in open boats for three months at sea.

Given the philosophical potential of the *Essex* story, it's perhaps surprising that more of the details didn't make it into Melville's novel: the nearest land from the spot of the attack was the Marquesas Islands, about 1,200 miles away, but the survivors feared being eaten by cannibals. Instead, they set out for South America, sailing an indirect route that covered some 4,000 miles. Only eight of the original twenty survived the voyage, surviving in part by eating seven of their shipmates—a diet high in both iron and irony.

Along with innumerable English-class snickers, *Moby-Dick* has also inspired a number of real-world enterprises:

- The Lake County Captains, a minor league baseball team near Cleveland, offer their fans a three-pound, twenty-dollar Moby Dick sandwich: five quarter-pound fish filets, eight slices of cheese, six ounces of clam strips, a third of a pound of fries, coleslaw, lettuce, tomato, and tartar sauce. Nothing on that sandwich is even a mammal, by the way, much less a whale.
- The musician Moby claims the author as his great-great grand uncle. Among Melville titles, he probably made the best choice of *nom de jam*—it would be hard to bliss out to the electronic stylings of DJ Bartleby the Scrivener.
- A certain coffee megachain is named for the chief mate in *Moby-Dick*. Why Starbucks does not offer anything called the "Mocha Dick," we may never know.

—A.W.

Q. Odlaw is the archnemesis of what kid-book character?

A. Waldo.

As a boy in 1960s London, Martin Handford always had an affinity for drawing crowd scenes; in one of his earliest drawings, he jammed a few hundred stick figures onto a single page. Art school didn't persuade him to concentrate on more traditional subjects, and that turned out well for the zeitgeist.

After Handford's first pass at a first book, his editors at Walker Books felt he needed a consistent, distinctive-looking character to search for in each illustration—those scenes filled with over three hundred figures needed at least *one more guy*. Handford gave that guy a red-and-white shirt and called him…Wally. That's still his name in the UK, but, you know, America gotta be different.

The people cluttering a Waldo page derive from Germany's *wimmelbilderbuch*, literally "teeming picture book." Designed in the sixties[1] to appeal to kids' frantic curiosity, *wimmel* pictures invite the viewer to break down the chaotic scene into smaller segments. The payoff is in finding the interesting tidbits placed throughout, instead of the zoomed-out cacophony. So, the actual finding of Waldo is merely a by-product—a journey, if you will, not a destination.[2]

---

1. Ultimately, it emulates the sixteenth-century stylings of famously weird Dutch painter Hieronymus Bosch. His magnum opus, *The Garden of Earthly Delights*, is crowded with severed ears, unicorns, and a naked dude riding a duck. If we had to stick Waldo in this triptych, we'd pick one of the (many) bizarre orgies in the middle panel.

2. Contrary to popular belief, that particular phrase has never been definitively attributed to R.W. Emerson. This is especially a shame for our purposes here—Emerson's friends all called him Waldo.

Anyway, the Waldo franchise hit its peak in the nineties with a barrage of activity books, video games, magazines, a comic strip, and an animated series, all based on the artwork of the seven O.G. books (Handford created his last original scene in 2009).[3] But the impact of Waldo lives on:

- In the aftermath of the 2008 subprime-mortgage crisis, Citigroup manager Brian Stoker beat fraud charges with the "*Where's Waldo* defense," i.e., that he was merely a minor player hidden among layers of senior management. Guess it's better than a Twinkie?
- In 2014, scientists developed a model of how cortical streams allow our brains to quickly search a scene and locate a target image. Their findings on the "Where's Waldo problem" were published in the medical journal *Frontiers in Integrative Neuroscience*.
- After skipping on a court appearance, a UK man made news in 2017 by evading his local constabulary for a whole weekend, taunting them with social media videos in which he dressed as Waldo. Perhaps not surprisingly for someone who chooses such a pastime, he eventually got bored and turned himself in.

Returning to our subject: dressed in nicely contrasting black and yellow, Waldo's semordnilap-tastic nemesis (look it up!) didn't appear until his fifth outing, *Where's Wally? The Magnificent Poster Book!* He was hell-bent on stealing our hero's walking stick—see, after the first three books took Waldo around the world, forward and backward in time, and even to pure fantasy lands, it became clear that the cane was a magical artifact.

None of this really explains why in his homeland, Wally's foe is still called Odlaw.

—B.C.

---

3. After milking Waldo dry in 2007, Handford had already sold the global merchandising rights for some $5 million US—hardly a Georgelucasian sum, but not bad for some jumped-up childhood doodles.

Q. In the novel *Catch-22*, what's the first name of Major Major?

A. Major.

Despite its unflinching gaze into the horrors of war, Joseph Heller's World War II satire makes most lists of the funniest books ever written. Its title worked its way into everyday language, describing a situation where the nature of a problem renders its only solution inherently unavailable: Orr the bomber pilot thinks he's mentally unfit to fly combat missions, so he asks for a mental evaluation. But the fact he's worried enough to ask means he's thinking clearly. Get back out there, flyboy!

The book's protagonist is John Yossarian, who is suitably impressed by the impossibility of his tentmate's situation. But we're here to talk about the real star: the father of Major Major M. Major,[1] a non-alfalfa farmer who hammers home the Catch-22 concept. "The more alfalfa he did not grow, the more money the government gave him," Heller writes, "and he spent every penny he didn't earn on new land to increase the amount of alfalfa he did not produce."

Like most satire, this isn't pure fiction. The US currently pays approximately $25 billion every year in subsidies to farmers, which have been included in every "Farm Bill" passed since the Great Depression, most recently in 2014.[2] The idea was sensibly sold as a promise that they could

---

1. The M stands for Major too. "A weaker man might have compromised on such excellent substitutes as Drum Major, Minor Major, Sergeant Major, or C. Sharp Major; but Major Major's father had waited fourteen years for just such an opportunity, and he was not a person to waste it."

2. After much bickering, Congress passed the most recent Farm Bill in December 2018. The hangup had to do with how little money they should give to poor people to buy food, because of course it did.

always support themselves, even in times of surplus; rather than make them incur all the costs of growing crops to be left to rot, it's cheaper to pay farmers to not grow the crops at all. And all this is well and good, but in oh-so-predictable practice, 85 percent of the subsidies go to the largest 15 percent of farm corporations. You're welcome, Big Ag!

"Catch-22" isn't the first expression in our language for a situation that's ironic—or otherwise unfortunate (see also the 1996 pop-culture case, *English teachers v. Morissette*). Consider, if you will:

- **"Damned if you do, damned if you don't,"** attributed to itinerant American preacher Lorenzo Dow.[3] He meant it literally—he was railing against other Christian leaders who, he said, had an unfortunate habit of twisting Scripture into contradictory positions. One presumes they would *not* be damned if they *didn't* do that, but Dow failed to clarify.
- **"Vicious circle,"** which dates to the late eighteenth century, and originally meant "a logical fallacy in which an argument assumes its own conclusion." This we know from eighteenth-century sources.
- **"Between the devil and the deep blue sea,"** which means the same thing as "a rock and a hard place" and the ancient Greeks' "Scylla and Charybdis," but is objectively the coolest of the three because of the devil, duh. Lorenzo Dow may disagree.

—T.C.

3. Also known as "Crazy Dow," the endearingly eccentric Lorenzo became something of a folk hero. On his death in 1834, a paper in one town he'd visited wrote, "Few who have seen him will forget his orangutan features, his outlandish clothes." *Damn.*

Q. What author's works have been adapted into the most films?

A. William Shakespeare.

Guinness World Records says there have been over 420 full-length movie or TV adaptations of the Bard's work, while *IMDb* credits him as a screenwriter on more than 1,400 productions. One of the very first was in 1899, and was actually a deep cut: four silent scenes from *King John* (yes, the same one who is a bad guy in *Robin Hood*).

Though it's not uncommon for Shakespeare adaptations to be nominated for Best Picture Oscars, and also not unusual for actors to be nominated for those works, it is surprisingly rare for these productions to *win*. The only real exception is the 1948 version of *Hamlet*, which won Best Picture and Best Actor.[1]

The 1990s saw a bumper crop of nominated *Hamlets*. Franco Zeffirelli's 1990 version starred Mel Gibson as the Danish prince, allegedly because the director was inspired (seriously) by Mel's suicidal turn in *Lethal Weapon*. Kenneth Branagh's 1996 production picked up four nods, or one for each hour of its running time.[2] With its fratricidal palace intrigue, even *The Lion King* has the whiff of rottenness in Denmark.

In fact, if we include movies that were merely *inspired* by the Bard, we can talk about several more Oscar winners—most famously *West Side Story*,

1. Laurence Olivier got his only competitive acting Oscar playing the title role, under his own direction. Clearly, the man was familiar with iambic pentameter: four of his eleven career acting nominations were for four different Shakespeare roles.

2. There were no nominations for Michael Almereyda's 2000 version, starring Ethan Hawke in then-modern-day New York, and setting the "to be or not to be" speech in a Blockbuster Video. (Kids: Blockbuster was sort of like if they put *Netflix* in a building you have to drive to.)

which roughly follows *Romeo and Juliet*,[3] but with lots more white people pretending to be Puerto Rican. And of course, there's *Shakespeare in Love*, a droll-enough fantasia revolving around the original production of *Romeo and Juliet*, but best remembered for stealing hardware from *Saving Private Ryan*.

If you want to find the very craziest adaptations this side of Stratford-upon-Avon, though, direct your attention to the small screen:

- In the *Gilligan's Island* episode "The Producer," the castaways try to showcase Ginger's acting skills by setting *Hamlet* to tunes from Bizet's famous opera *Carmen*, with Gilligan in the title role (Hamlet, not Carmen). "To be or not to be" becomes the famous "Habanera," and Polonius's "Neither a borrower nor a lender be" is sung by the Skipper as "The Toreador Song." This was the same decade as *The Flying Nun* and *My Mother the Car*, so it's best not to question too much.

- The *Moonlighting* episode "Atomic Shakespeare" is framed as the daydream of a young *Moonlighting* fan who reads *The Taming of the Shrew* while picturing his favorite TV characters. Playing Petruchio, Bruce Willis makes his big entrance on horseback—the rider and his mount both wearing shades. In 2009, *TV Guide* called it one of the fifty best episodes of any show ever, sunglasses-horse or nay.

- And of course *The Simpsons* did it; the season thirteen episode "Tales from the Public Domain" has Bart as (yet again) Hamlet. Sure enough, everybody dies in the end, including RosenCarl and GuildenLenny. Even so, Bart would apparently rather watch *NYPD Blue*: "Steven Bochco could kick Shakespeare's ass."

—P.S.P.

---

3. Not everybody was impressed: as critic Pauline Kael famously said, "First you take Shakespeare's *Romeo and Juliet*, and remove all that cumbersome poetry."

Q. Marvel's Daredevil mostly prowls around what Manhattan neighborhood?

A. Hell's Kitchen.

New Yorkers had a good laugh when *Marvel's Daredevil* appeared on *Netflix* in 2015. Blind attorney Matt Murdock, "The Devil of Hell's Kitchen," haunts the rooftops of a crime-ridden neighborhood, its ethnic residents endlessly harassed by corrupt ethnic gangs. Maybe that was true once, but now Hell's Kitchen[1]—basically Midtown west of Seventh Avenue—is mostly known as the site of fancy restaurants, *The Daily Show* tapings, and the Holland Tunnel.

When *Daredevil* was created in 1964 by Stan Lee and Bill Everett (and probably Jack Kirby), Hell's Kitchen was a very different kind of place. For one hundred years, the Kitchen mostly housed Irish dockworkers, their families, and the dive bars that kept them lubricated, all ruled over by more-terrifying-than-they-sound street gangs like the Gophers and Westies.

By the sixties, the dock jobs had faded, leaving only decaying tenements and despair. An Irish mobster ruled the neighborhood, controlling gambling rackets and a half dozen nightclubs; Mickey Spillane[2] was so tough that he held members of La Cosa Nostra for ransom. In the real world it was definitely the kind of neighborhood that needed saving.

---

1. Though it's undeniably bad-ass, the origin of the name Hell's Kitchen is unclear. Some attribute it to a quote from Davy Crockett, others to a less-famous character named "Dutch Fred the Cop." In 1881 *The New York Times* called it "probably the lowest and filthiest" of the city's neighborhoods—and Port Authority hadn't even been *built* yet.

2. Not to be confused with the prolific crime novelist, who created Mike Hammer, used the phrase "stark naked" a lot, became a Jehovah's Witness, hung out with Ayn Rand, died in 2006, and still has books on the way.

So not-real Matt Murdock was raised there by his boxer dad, who implored him to be an egghead rather than a jock (the neighborhood kids sarcastically call him "Daredevil"). While trying to push a blind man out of the way of an oncoming truck, Matt gets exposed to a radioactive substance that blinds him, but heightens his other senses and gives him a "radar sense." He uses these to battle an Irish mobster named "The Fixer," who had his father killed for refusing to throw a fight.

It's all pretty reminiscent of that other quintessentially Manhattan hero, Spider-Man. But it's fun! Just consider these goofy Silver Age villains he fought:

- **Gladiator.** A disgraced costume designer who builds a suit of armor because he wants to be tougher than Daredevil. "Fool! Why do you prolong your agony?" he says, right before getting his ass kicked.
- **Stilt-Man.** A disgraced engineer who becomes a supervillain after inventing a pair of hydraulic metal legs. In his first fight with Daredevil, he gets shrunk to microscopic size. Why not?
- **Leap-Frog.** A disgraced toy inventor who develops a metallic frog exoskeleton that allows him to leap great distances. He, um, also loses.

The Daredevil we know today looks more like Frank Miller's gritty 1980s take, in which he tries to stop the Kingpin from turning Hell's Kitchen into a global center for organized crime.[3] In his law practice, Murdock also tries to protect the little people from Kingpin's evil ways, but rarely succeeds. Cue the moody rooftop lurking!

—N.P.

3. In 1972 he moved to San Francisco, where he lived platonically in a mansion with the Black Widow—the first Marvel heroes on the West Coast. Murdock remained in the mansion for twenty issues, and he's bounced back and forth since then. Regardless, wherever Daredevil goes, gentrification is sure to follow.

Q. Reaching all the way back to childhood, Arnold Schwarzenegger's 2012 memoir had what title?

A. Total Recall.

Based on Philip K. Dick's short story "We Can Remember It for You Wholesale," *Total Recall*, with its mysterious memory-chip implants, is one of the many Dick works that showcases his unusual view of reality. As a young man, he became convinced there was no way to confirm that reality is actually real, a philosophy that may have provided some solace in what was a decidedly rocky life.

Dick struggled to make it as a conventional novelist for more than a decade until 1963, when *The Man in the High Castle* won the Hugo Award for Best Novel. But he still had a hard time making ends meet, took too much speed, and saw his fourth marriage fall apart in 1972, leading to a suicide attempt. Two years after *that*, Dick had a series of religious and paranormal hallucinations—that the Roman Empire had been reborn in the Nixon administration, for instance, and was responsible for all those assassinations in the sixties—then lost his connection to that extraterrestrial information portal, and tried to kill himself again.

He didn't seek treatment for a stroke in 1982 and died that March,[1] just fifty-three years old.

In his amphetamine-fueled thirty-year career, Dick wrote forty-four novels and more than one hundred short stories. In the decades since his death, he's become a bona fide Hollywood darling:

---

1. Well, he lives on in a more literal sense than most authors: In 2006 a robotic Dick simulacrum was supposed to answer questions about the film adaptation of *A Scanner Darkly* at San Diego Comic-Con. But an airline employee accidentally lost its head, which was never found. Have you seen that Dick head? (Sorry, we had to do one.)

- ***Blade Runner***, based on his story "Do Androids Dream of Electric Sheep?" was released later in 1982.[2] Starring a white-hot Harrison Ford, it met immediate commercial and critical disinterest, but is now in *IMDb*'s Top 250 list of history's best-loved movies.
- Steven Spielberg's 2002 film ***Minority Report*** starred Tom Cruise as a "pre-crime" detective, trying to solve a murder he himself has been apprehended for, of a man he doesn't know, before he's committed the allegedly forthcoming crime.
- In 2015, Dick's breakthrough novel, ***The Man in the High Castle***, was loosely adapted into an Amazon TV series in which Germany and Japan have divvied up the United States after winning World War II—except some people in the Underground have stumbled upon film evidence of another, more familiar-to-us timeline. Standard stuff, in other words.

Then there's *Total Recall*, the 1990 movie starring Arnold Schwarzenegger,[3] at the height of his pre-governator fame. His character gets a video message from himself, saying all his memories are bogus implants, but that turns out to be part of a lie that the *old* him told his *future* self, in order to destroy the local resistance to a Martian despot. And in the end, the whole thing might've been a dream. Or not! But maybe!

Unsurprisingly, Arnold's memoir was much more straightforward.

—P.S.P.

2. It was set in 2019, so let's check the scoreboard. We don't have flying cars or android replicants—or Pan Am, for that matter—but we do have computers we can talk to, and video chat. Not bad!

3. And a less-essential 2012 remake. Costar Jessica Biel insisted the do-over hewed closer to Dick's original story, which may be *sorta* true—but as it happens, her own character appears *only* in the 1990 film, not the story.

Q. What are the first and middle names of A.A. Milne's son?

A. Christopher Robin.

And what would C.R. Milne have preferred as the name for the only human denizen of the Hundred Acre Wood? Literally anything else. The bullying he suffered, he said, made the books—*Winnie-the-Pooh* (1926) and *The House at Pooh Corner* (1928)—a source of "toe-curling, fist-clenching, lip-biting embarrassment." He finally made peace with it in his later years, before dying in 1996.

Anyway, let's talk about something sunnier: the whole media property stemming from those books, which are hilarious and charming and hardly fist-clenching at all. The original animals, owned in real life by Christopher Robin, included Tigger, Kanga, Eeyore, Piglet, and…Edward Bear.[1] He already bore that name when Alan Alexander bought him for Christopher's first birthday, but he was quickly renamed "Winnie," after the boy's favorite bear at the London Zoo. The "Pooh" part came from Chris himself, who once bestowed that name on a random swan. If you've ever had nightmares about a bear-swan chimera, now you know why.

Most of the other characters' names are pretty obvious.[2] And no, the original stuffed Pooh didn't hang with Rabbit and Owl, but A.A. decided

1. These animals can be visited at the New York Public Library on 42nd Street, because a grown-up Christopher gave them to the US publisher in 1947, and that publisher then donated them to the library. Obviously, some Britons want them back—Tony Blair is rumored to have once asked Bill Clinton about it.

2. "Eeyore," with that non-rhotic British *r* sound, is how you say "hee-haw" in England. Bonus joke for our older readers: *The Benny Hill Show* is another way to say "Hee Haw" in England.

the Hundred Acre Wood needed a total crank and an insufferable know-it-all. Who needs enemies?

The forgotten name in this story is Stephen Slesinger, the father of modern licensing rights who also made a jungle of cash with the Tarzan character, and created the famed Red Ryder BB Gun. Slesinger bought Pooh's North American merchandising and media rights for the inflation-adjusted 1930 equivalent of $15,000 (and a third of the royalties). He started up a cottage industry of dolls, records, board games…you get the picture. Within two years, Depression be damned, the property was worth more like $800 *million*.

When Slesinger died in 1953, Disney swooped in and took the stories global.[3] Through the years, many notable people have voiced the iconic characters, including:

- **Paul Winchell**, the voice of Tigger until the 1990s. He rose to fame as a ventriloquist, with his dummy Jerry Mahoney. He also—this is true—held the first patent on an artificial heart, which sadly could not bring Jerry to life.
- **Kristen Anderson-Lopez**, the voice of Kanga in the 2011 movie. She has Oscars for cowriting "Let It Go" from *Frozen* and "Remember Me" from *Coco*; with an addition of an Emmy and a Tony, she can join her husband, Robert, on the EGOT (Emmy, Grammy, Oscar, Tony) list.
- **Clint Howard**, Ron's brother and acting-credit hog (248 on *IMDb*, as of this writing). At age seven, he originated Disney's Roo; by the time he had to re-create the role in 1977, for *The Many Adventures of Winnie the Pooh*, he was seventeen. If only Paul Winchell had invented puberty reversal!

—S.B.

3. Especially in Japan: the hottest ride at Tokyo Disneyland's Fantasyland is Pooh's Hunny Hunt, and Pooh-branded honey popcorn once created a beekeeping boom. If you balk at *Variety*'s assertion that Pooh is Disney's most lucrative character, you're just on the wrong side of the world.

Q. The Greek god Pan is usually pictured carrying what musical instrument?

A. Pan flute.

Even casual Hellenophiles could pick Pan out of a lineup: sexy horned dude on top, goat on the bottom—basically classic Satan, without the lame pentagram tattoos. The son of a human goatherd who tended his flock a little *too* closely, Pan has the modern reputation of a fancy-free gadabout, harmlessly strolling the countryside like a mutant Johnny Appleseed. The truth, however, is that Pan was a hoofed harbinger of horror worse than Zeus, Hades, and that one really snidey Argonaut combined.

As a god of the wild, Pan generally spent his days dozing outdoors,[1] and his nights lusting after nature spirits called nymphs, most of whom didn't give a bent drachma for his woolly ass. These one-sided courtships mostly ended with the unlucky nymphs getting transformed into stuff: Echo became a disembodied voice, Pitys a fir tree, and the forest spirit Syrinx a patch of reeds, which Pan bound together to make his trademark pipes. What a romantic!

True to form, our goatish friend used his grisly new instrument to spiral the lives of every poor sod who ran into him. The infamous King Midas said he preferred Pan's rustic tootings to Apollo's snooty lyre-work; the jealous sun god tacked some donkey ears on to his golden-touch curse. The herdsman Daphnis went to Pan for flute lessons and wound up getting blinded by his girlfriend and plunging off a cliff. Benedict Arnold heard him playing at a bar, and decided to surrender West Point to the damnable redcoats... okay, we made that last one up, but you're seeing a pattern here, right?

---

1. Woe betide anyone who interrupted Pan's afternoon power naps. He'd immediately launch into a screaming magical hissy fit, striking the offending mortals mad with terror—hence the word *panic*.

Nowadays "pan flute" refers to a whole international family of mouth organs, and surprise! They're still a font of misfortune and anguish. Just consider this short list of famous panpipe fans:

- Cleopatra's dad, Pharaoh **Ptolemy XII** of Egypt, called "the flautist" because he preferred jamming to, say, ruling effectively. He got deposed and had to pay the Roman Empire a ludicrous sum to take his throne back, whereupon he executed the (non-Cleopatra) daughter who had succeeded him.[2]
- Explorer **James Cook**, who in 1771 brought back some Polynesian-style pipes from his first South Pacific voyage. Two trips later, Cook took a Hawaiian king hostage and caught a fatal shanking for his trouble.
- **Papageno**, the bass-singing birdman from Mozart's weird final opera, *The Magic Flute*. His role is to completely ignore all the specific moral instructions given to him by the supernatural forces guiding the action, and get everything he wants anyway—all while incessantly playing do-re-mi-fa-so on his panpipes.[3] So where's the calamity? He often takes his last bow with a gaggle of small children he's just fathered. Kids, am I right?

Nowadays the Romanians, of all people, are keeping the pan-flute hype alive through a curvy local version called a *nai*. Bucharest-born Simion Stanciu even contributed his legendary skills to albums by Yes and The Moody Blues. If that's not continuing a legacy of misery, we don't know what is.

—E.K.

2. Because the Egyptians liked marrying pharaohs off to siblings, that murdered daughter was probably also his niece. Soak it in, *Game of Thrones* fans.

3. They aren't the titular instrument, by the way. That would be the regular straight flute bestowed upon the hero Tamino, who meticulously follows all the instructions, and is rewarded by literally having to trek through hell.

Geeks Who Drink Presents: Duh!

Q. J.M. Barrie donated the copyright for *Peter Pan* to what particular type of hospital?

D.H. Lawrence once said, "J.M. Barrie has a fatal touch for those he loves." Just like when he figured people would want to read about Lady Chatterley getting it on with her gamekeeper, Lawrence was not wrong. Pour a stiff drink and think happy thoughts—it's gonna be a rough one.

Tragedy came early for young James Matthew. His beloved older brother David died in a skating accident, a day shy of his fourteenth birthday. David was known to be their mother's favorite; overcome with grief, she wouldn't leave her room. To console her, the six-year-old J.M. imitated his dead brother, clothes and all. Thankfully, the episode instilled a love of theater in the lad, rather than Norman Bates–style murder.

In the late 1890s, a childless, thirty-something Barrie met the Llewelyn Davies boys in Kensington Gardens and formed a fast friendship. When their mother, Sylvia, recognized him at a party as the same tiny Scottish man her sons had told her so much about, she was surprisingly chill about it. His relations with the family inspired his hit 1904 play, *Peter Pan*.[1]

Mind you, this whole time Barrie was married to somebody else, an actress named Mary Ansell. There's no evidence that his friendship with Sylvia was anything more than platonic—though after Mr. Llewelyn Davies died of facial cancer at forty-four, Barrie bought the family a house. Anyway, shortly after that, Mary divorced Barrie after falling in love with

---

1. This friendship also inspired the 2004 movie *Finding Neverland*, starring Johnny Depp and Kate Winslet. But some of the facts were fudged to keep the movie from being heinously depressing. The result was what the *London Evening Standard* called "neutered whimsy."

a much younger writer.[2] And shortly after *that*, Sylvia died of lung cancer at forty-three. Drink!

Barrie then adopted the five Davies boys, maybe even forging documents to make it happen. Possible felonies notwithstanding, you might think the idea of orphans finding a home with their loving father figure constitutes a happy ending. Smash cut to montage:

- **George Llewelyn Davies** was killed in the First World War, at age twenty-one.
- **Michael Llewelyn Davies** drowned in 1921, age twenty, while attending Oxford. He died alongside a male classmate, leading to speculation that they were lovers in a suicide pact. Much like his mother, Barrie never fully recovered from the loss of his favorite child.[3]
- **Peter Llewelyn Davies** came home from the Great War with severe shell shock. He published books by his cousin Daphne du Maurier, of *Rebecca* fame, and made it all the way to sixty-three before throwing himself in front of a Tube train.

J.M. Barrie, at least, wasn't around to see Peter's tragic end. He died of blessedly natural causes in 1937, just past his seventy-seventh birthday, donating all *Peter Pan* rights and royalties to London's Great Ormond Street Hospital for Children. He stipulated that the amount of the annuity was never to be disclosed, but that it was to continue indefinitely.

Don't worry—as of this writing, the hospital's still going strong.

—L.T.

2. Even after she married her backdoor man, Mary largely lived off of support checks from J.M.—which he handed over at annual dinners held on their original anniversary. My *dude*.

3. He couldn't even remember him by visiting the still-standing 1912 *Peter Pan* statue he'd commissioned in Kensington Gardens. He wanted it to be modeled after Michael, but the sculptor chose another boy.

Q. What novel did Dostoevsky write to pay off his gambling debts?

A. The Gambler.

In 1863 a forty-something Fyodor Dostoevsky was on holiday in the western German resort town of Wiesbaden, when he sat down at a roulette table. No one ever wins at roulette, and he was no exception—but like so many before and since, that didn't stop him from getting hooked.

A couple of years later, Dostoevsky signed a Faustian publishing contract with a fellow Fyodor, F.T. Stellovsky. Dostoevsky got a big enough advance to keep creditors at bay, but, according to the contract, if he didn't produce a book by November 1, 1866, Stellovsky would own everything he wrote for the next nine years. Courtesy of *The Dostoevsky Encyclopedia*,[1] the next stretch looked like this: burn drafts of *Crime and Punishment*, get rejected by a woman almost twenty years his junior, lose at roulette, hit the pawn shop, couch-surf with a buddy, get hassled by brother's family for money, repeat.

In October 1866, with nothing written and a deadline seriously looming, Dostoevsky's romantic *and* professional luck turned when he hired twenty-year-old stenographer Anna Snitkina. The exact details of the next twenty-six days are murky, but apparently Anna lit a fire under his ass. He managed to complete *The Gambler*[2] on deadline and, unable to reach Stellovsky on November 1, got the date certified by the local police. Keep your receipts!

---

1. You know you've made it when there's a whole encyclopedia about you. Just ask the subject of *A Theodore Dreiser Encyclopedia*—which, oddly enough, is Broadway legend Chita Rivera (not really).

2. Working title: *Roulettenburg*, which is a bit like if Stephen King's *It* were called *Clown Town*.

Finished with the novel, and just shy of his forty-fifth birthday, Dostoevsky worried about losing Anna. Rather than just come out and say he liked her, Dostoevsky tried to pick her up by making her a female-psychology consultant on his new novel, in which an elderly artist wishes to propose to a younger woman named Anya. Sure enough, this whole Russian Nora Ephron routine turned into an actual proposal. Anna said *da*, and just like a Harry vis-à-vis Sally, Fyodor probably got the better end of the deal—she wrote his definitive biography, twice.[3]

Ironically, Fyodor's gambling addiction was further fueled by the successful completion of *The Gambler*; the couple still had several bankruptcies ahead of them. His family insists that he did eventually conquer his problem, though, and in fact sued Russia's nationwide sports lottery after they saw fit to use Dostoevsky's likeness on a 2004 scratch-off ticket.

A few more facts about roulette that are more fun than playing roulette:

- Mathematician Blaise Pascal is credited with inventing what would become the modern roulette wheel, while working on an idea for a perpetual motion machine. He's also the creator of "Pascal's Wager," the idea that you bet on God's existence with your very life. Neither thing is very mathematical, now that we think about it.
- In the 1860s, France's Blanc brothers, who'd popularized European roulette, helped Prince Charles III pull Monaco out of crushing debt by running Monte Carlo's first modern casino. Since then, the principality has been characterized by a much more upscale seediness. *No one needs that many Lamborghinis.*
- You've heard that roulette is the worst bet in the house, but the extra 00 space on an American wheel gives the house an even bigger edge than in European roulette. USA! USA!

—J.H.G.

---

3. Inspired by her husband's snide remark about female flakiness, Anna also became the first female Russian stamp collector. This was probably more impressive than it sounds.

Q. In the Harry Potter books, Professor Lupin is what sort of monster?

A. Werewolf.

Spellbinding storyteller though she is, J.K. Rowling generally is not subtle with her foreshadowing. "Lupin" isn't even the only wolf indicator in the name of Harry's third-year Defense Against the Dark Arts teacher; his first name, Remus, is an homage to the mythical twins who founded Rome.[1] Introduced in *Harry Potter and the Prisoner of Azkaban*, the professor comes to be a trusted friend and mentor to Harry Potter, as he was a classmate and friend of Harry's late father, James; he's finally "revealed" as a werewolf by the always-observant Hermione in chapter seventeen.

Rowling has said that Lupin's lycanthropy was a metaphor for illnesses with societal stigma, such as AIDS. Other fictional universes have taken it much lighter, using werewolves as a super-fun puberty metaphor:

- In the 1985 movie *Teen Wolf*, Scott's lupine tendencies popped up (so to speak) when he was sexually aroused. At one point his dad confronts him about his condition while Scott is locked in the bathroom, then they have a talk about his changing body and how it's totally normal. It's all Very Special.

---

1. In the legend of Romulus and Remus, the (human) newborns escaped a royal infanticide mandate by getting floated down the River Tiber in a basket. If that sounds like the Moses story, it is—up until they're rescued by a she-wolf, who nurses them with her eight giant teats, in a kinda-startling statue that can still be seen all over the Roman ruins of Europe. Incidentally, in *Harry Potter and the Deathly Hallows*, when everyone's lives were constantly in danger, Remus Lupin used "Romulus" as his code name. If wizards had online banking, we're pretty sure his password would be "password."

- In *Buffy the Vampire Slayer*, most everything is a teen-sex metaphor. Take Seth Green's adorable werewolf Daniel "Oz" Osbourne, who understandably fears that the heroes will silver-bullet his ass, and thus hides his new nocturnal condition…in the very same episode that introduces a closeted gay character. Never fear, though: Oz remains un-slayed, and is assured by his girlfriend, Willow— who also later comes out as gay—that "three days out of the month, I'm not much fun to be around either."
- Did someone make a menses joke? In the 2000 Canadian cult classic *Ginger Snaps* the protagonist, Ginger (duh), gets bitten by a werewolf on the very same night as her first period. It's all very confusing for her, as we suppose it would be. "I get this ache," she says. "I thought it was for sex, but it's to tear everything to fucking pieces."

Lupin came onto the scene when the main Potter characters were all turning thirteen, and evidently Rowling thought it a bit early to hit those notes;[2] she waited two more books before pairing off all the hormonal students.

And Lupin *left* the scene in the traumatic, series-ending Battle of Hogwarts. Rowling has told readers that the death scene made her cry because she loves the character so much. She even apologized to fans on the "anniversary" of the battle, saying the only reason Lupin had to die was because Arthur Weasley lived, and she wanted to take out as many parents as possible— especially Harry's father figures.[3]

In other words, her apologies are exactly as masterful as her foreshadowing.

—L.T.

2. Lupin's friends call his lycanthropy a "furry little problem," which at least *sounds* pubescent.

3. She further explained that she was just trying to be realistic about the horrors of war, but… you okay, J.K.?

Q. Mark Twain grew up on what river?

A. The Mississippi.

Twain was born Samuel Clemens under Halley's Comet in 1835, in the tiny landlocked hamlet of Florida, Missouri.[1] He was four when his family famously moved some 40 miles to slightly larger Hannibal, which, along with the mighty Mississippi River on which it squats, served as the setting for *The Adventures of Tom Sawyer* and *The Adventures of Huckleberry Finn*.[2] In other words, he had one of the best-documented childhoods in American history:

- His mother, **Jane Clemens**, served as the basis for Aunt Polly. A true Southern belle, Mrs. Clemens loved parades and parties, hated housekeeping, and often would bring home strangers from the market for lemonade and socializing.
- Becky Thatcher was inspired by his childhood sweetheart, **Laura Hawkins**, who lived right across the street. They remained friends throughout their lives, and they were honored together at a dinner in Hannibal just before Twain's death. When Hawkins died in 1928, she merited a full-column obituary in *The New York Times*.

---

1. Epilogue: Its arable farmland disappeared in the mid-1960s—flooded away, ironically, by the construction of Mark Twain Lake. Twain's birthplace is intact as part of a historical site and museum, but as of the 2010 census, the town of Florida had an official population of zero.

2. In the books, he called Hannibal "St. Petersburg," but Cardiff Hill, the islands, and the big cave south of town all actually exist. That whitewashed fence they have now? Totally fake.

- A kid named **Tom Blankenship** gave him the idea for Huckleberry Finn. In his autobiography, Twain said that Blankenship was "ignorant, unwashed, insufficiently fed," but "had as good a heart as ever any boy had." The last Twain had heard, Blankenship was a justice of the peace in a remote Montana village. History has not recorded whether he ever took up rafting.

At any rate, in 1857, young Sam Clemens was on assignment to write local color for an Iowa newspaper called the *Keokuk Daily Post*. But he finally succumbed to the call of the Mississippi and decided to become a riverboat pilot instead.[3] In the two years it took Clemens to get his license, his brother Henry also went to work on the river, but he died when his steamboat exploded in 1858. The elder brother blamed himself for the rest of his life, but continued to work the almost 2,500 miles of the Mississippi until 1861, when service was disrupted by the stark inconvenience of a great civil war.

But by that point the legend was well underway. River men yelled "mark twain" to indicate that the water depth was 2 fathoms, or 12 feet, and therefore safe to navigate; after resuming his writing career, Clemens thought it would make a good enough byline for a humorous travel story—and most everything else he would ever write. He died under Halley's Comet, in faraway Connecticut, in 1910.

Twain never did go back to piloting, but that part of his career lives on in the *Mark Twain Riverboat*, which has been offering a dinner buffet cruise from the Hannibal docks for more than thirty years. A big eater himself, and the subject of an entire 2011 book called *Twain's Feast*, the author might well have approved of this development. Or maybe he'd bail and go explore a cave with Becky Thatcher.

—N.P.

---

3. It helped that the job paid $250 a month, a huge sum for the time—certainly better than freelance writing, then or now.

Q. Marvel superhero Namor the Sub-Mariner has a name inspired by what ancient civilization?

A. Roman.

Often called Marvel's first superhero, Namor was created by Bill Everett for *Motion Picture Funnies Weekly*, a comic designed for free distribution in movie theaters.[1] Everett picked the name by…well, by randomly picking the word *Roman* and turning it backward, because he thought it looked cool.[2]

The half-human ruler of Atlantis, Namor can command fish telepathically (at least sometimes—you know how loose comic-book continuity is). So, he's just an Aquaman rip-off, right? Well, no. It's not that Marvel was *never* "inspired" by already-existing DC heroes—see Hawkeye versus Green Arrow, Quicksilver versus Flash, etc.—but Namor dates to 1939, a full two years *before* Aquaman's debut. Besides, they're totally different: Namor can fly, defying all laws of aerodynamics, thanks to some tiny wings on his ankles.[3]

1. If this sounds like a terrible business model, yup! The book barely even made it past the prototype stage, so now Namor's first appearance is generally credited as the later-in-1939 premiere of *Marvel Comics*—the Timely Comics series they liked so much, they wound up naming the whole company for it.

2. The also-dumb name "Sub-Mariner" was an homage to Samuel Taylor Coleridge's "The Rime of the Ancient Mariner" and not that Rolex that James Bond used to wear. That watch didn't hit shelves until 1953—but, late or not, history has shown it was a much better idea than *Motion Picture Funnies Weekly*.

3. He was likely the first flying superhero (remember, Superman could only "leap tall buildings"), but the ankle wings straight-up don't make sense for an aquatic super. That's why Marvel eventually retconned Namor into the "first mutant"—a distinction that's only *partly* true, and only in *our* universe. His mutanthood was established in the 1960s by the already-mutant X-Men, and there are several older in-universe mutants (Selene, for example, is seventeen thousand years young).

Namor also has a sheer badassery advantage over Aquaman, who needed help from Jason Momoa to finally end his lame streak. Namor started out as the villain you're cheering for, sort of an underwater Walter White. For example, he first met the O.G. Human Torch while trying to tidal-wave Manhattan. After World War II he switched sides to fight the Nazis, then faded into obscurity and cancellation—like Captain America, only without the successful revivals, Chris Evans dreamboat factor, and catchy logo that serves as a license to print merch money.

So yes, Namor is firmly on Marvel's B-team. But that hasn't stopped them from making two freakin' Ant-Man movies (so far), so where's the Namor love? Surprisingly, Hollywood has talked about this since the nineties— but that was also the time Marvel was farming off heroes to other studios, so Namor is stuck in the same legal limbo that's keeping Dr. Bruce Banner from headlining another film. HULK SMASH PUNY CONTRACT LAW!

One of the ways Marvel has kept Namor in the picture lately was the Illuminati. No, he's not in the historical Bavarian outfit that weirdo seventies stoners wouldn't shut up about, but a totally different secret organization meant to…guide superhero policy, or something. It never has made much sense. Anyway, other members include:

- **Professor Charles Xavier**, representing the X-Men, and also overwrought tolerance metaphors.
- **Iron Man**, representing the Avengers, and also billionaires (which is admittedly handy).
- **Doctor Strange**, representing his weird self, and also vaguely racist origin stories. Really, Marvel? An ancient master at "a hidden temple somewhere in the remote vastness of Asia"?

—P.S.P.

Q. What's the last word of the King James Version of the Bible?

A. Amen.

Amen is a rare word that has been used almost exactly the same way for some three millennia. It comes from ancient Hebrew, where it variously meant "to support, to believe, or be faithful." If there were Israelite rappers, we can be pretty sure they would have said "amen" instead of "word."[1]

Reading the Bible from the top, the first "amen" is in Numbers 5, in a distinctly Old Testament adultery test—for women only, natch. Basically, your priest will tell your wife to drink some holy water he has just dirtied up. If she's lying about her fidelity, her womb will waste away on the spot. The woman's response is to be "Amen, amen"—and honestly, what else is there to say at that point?[2]

In the New Testament, Paul and his fellow epistle-writers used it at the end of prayers—and just like today, they expected you to say it back. In First Corinthians, Paul says you shouldn't pray in tongues, because "how can an outsider say 'Amen' if he doesn't know what you're talking about?" Word.

---

1. And they would have said it "ah-main." Latin turned it to "ah-men," then it became "ay-men" after medieval England's Great Vowel Shift. That was a complex and super-mysterious change that affected all of English, and the reason why it's so weird to hear an expert read Chaucer. So why do some Christians still say "ah-men"? According to the linguists we asked, that's basically just because Latin makes you sound smart.

2. The Sixth Amendment to the US Constitution, guaranteeing the right to an attorney, would not be ratified until 1791.

As for Revelation—not only the last book of the Bible, but also the last *added* to the Bible[3]—it does in fact end with a hearty "The grace of the Lord Jesus Christ be with you all, amen."

Since the first century, the word has turned up in some disparate phrases:

- The beautiful **Amen glass** was a sort of eighteenth-century campaign button, supporting the British pretender James III. About forty examples remain of the drinking glass, inscribed with the then-new lyrics of "God Save the King," followed by our (almost) favorite four-letter word.
- The **amen corner** is the part of a US church sanctuary, mostly in the South, where the worshippers most loudly and frequently agree with the preacher. Can I get a witness?
- History's most famous 6 seconds of drumming, the **Amen break** was lifted from a 1969 funk-gospel cover by The Winstons. That breakbeat—boom boom TAH, boom buh-boom TAH—was later sampled in at least 1,500 songs, from "Straight Outta Compton" to the *Futurama* theme. You just know those ancient Jewish rappers would have used it too.

Back in Israel, the Jewish people never forgot their most enduring contribution to world language. At the 1995 Eurovision Song Contest, Ashkelon-born Liora Fadlon entered a world-peace ballad called "Amen." It came in eighth.

—C.D.S.

3. Yes, early Christians knew John's Revelation was weird, with its seven-headed beasts and 666 shenanigans. According to a third-century critic, "The title is fraudulent....It is not the work of John, nor is it a revelation, because it is covered thickly and densely by a veil of obscurity." Burn? But in the 400s it was finally accepted into canon, and the rival Apocalypse of Peter left out; consequently, we'll have to wait and see if, as revealed to Peter, blasphemers really spend eternity hanging by their tongues.

Acknowledgments

First things first: my family supported me a great deal throughout this quick, crazy process. Everyone says that, but it has to be true or else nothing can happen. Thankfully, it *is* true.

Of course, two other people had to believe in the book before it could land in your hands: Murray Weiss at Catalyst Literary Management, and Eileen Mullan at Adams Media. Neal Pollack helped me get the ball rolling in their direction.

When the facts took me beyond my ability to competently edit them—or, at least, when I *recognized* that was happening—I called in expertise from friends and professors, and professors who are friends. They can decide which category they're in. Anyway, thanks to Steve Bahnaman, Jim Brown, Jeremy Hartnett, Nicole Holliday, Daniel Petrie, Nick Rogers, Ann Taylor, Will Turner, and Julie Wolfson, this book is more insightful and less inaccurate than it might have been.

Geeks Who Drink's art director, Holland Hume, threw down those righteous front cover illustrations. John Dicker hired me, gave advice when I asked (and only when I asked!), and otherwise just handed me the brand to run off with in this strange direction. And then there are three people whose bios appear here, but who helped develop this concept and format when we were trying to figure out just what it was, and offered tons of help along the way: Bryan Carr, Eric Keihl, and *my* original quizmaster, Aaron Retka.

Thanks, everybody!
—C.D.S.

About Geeks Who Drink

Formed in Denver in 2006, Geeks Who Drink emerged with a few other trends in American life: the rising tide of craft beer, the passage of smoking bans in bars and restaurants, and the emergence of social media. Played in one thousand bars nationwide, our live-hosted quiz runs six days a week. We run monthly theme quizzes, giving a chance for major pop-culture nerds to do deep dives on their favorite fandoms. But our signature event is Geek Bowl, the annual traveling championship that draws hundreds of teams to compete for thousands of dollars in cash—and to experience the world's most lavish trivia production and the cleverest questions our writing crew can wring out of their mind grapes.

Geeks Who Drink Writers

Steve Bahnaman is a former Geek Bowl champion and college librarian. In 2015 he was the biggest winner on the nearly forgotten ABC quiz show *500 Questions*. He lives with his wife, Sarah Stanley, and children, Miles and Lucy, in Raleigh, North Carolina.

Bryan Carr won his third-grade class spelling bee. When he's not busy as a Geeks Who Drink editor, he works in business development for a manufacturing company in St. Louis, where he lives with his wife, Danielle.

Tyler Crosby is a museum educator by day, and a writer/quizmaster by night. A former contestant on *Who Wants to Be a Millionaire?* (won a bunch of money) and *Jeopardy!* (not so much), he lives with his partner, Meghan, and cat, Garnet, in Boston.

Jonpaul Henry Guinn is a Geeks Who Drink staff writer and quizmaster, a *Jeopardy!* also-ran, and a US Army veteran. He lives in Austin, Texas.

Nicole Holliday is a linguistics professor in Los Angeles. A quizmaster since 2014, and question-writer since 2016, she has also appeared on *Who Wants to Be a Millionaire?* and *The Chase*. Someday she'll finally win the big money!

Eric Keihl brilliantly leveraged a 2008 College Bowl national championship into an overnight clerk job at 7-Eleven. Now an editor for Geeks Who Drink, he lives with his girlfriend and his three cats in Pittsburgh.

Lea M. Popielinski became a Geeks Who Drink editor after years working as an academic editor and writing virtual-world quizzes. Besides her doctoral dissertation, on gender and sexuality in virtual worlds, she has also published a couple of chapters in academic anthologies. She lives with her partner, Beverly, and Bev's kids in North Carolina.

Aaron Retka is managing editor of Geeks Who Drink, former editor and publisher of the alt-monthly *Newspeak*, and an SPJ awardee whose work has appeared in a literal smattering of dailies and alt-weeklies nationwide. He lives in Colorado with his wife, his squirrelly ass children, and too many fish tanks. He's not on *Twitter*, so please stop asking.

Matthew Sherman is an Emmy-nominated writer of trivia questions for TV shows, pub quizzes, and mobile games. He lives with his wife, Andrea, and their sons, Eli and Arlo, in Culver City, California.

Lindsay Thobe is a quizmaster who has performed stand-up at the Chicago Women's Funny Festival. Born in New Bremen, Ohio, she has lived in Chicago for the past ten years, cohabitating with three plants and a cardboard cutout of Benedict Cumberbatch.

John Tullar has put a solid 67 percent effort into the hundreds of questions he's penned for Geeks Who Drink. Originally from Tucson, Arizona, he mostly lives around Boston these days, when he's not at his second home on that Brazilian island that's covered with snakes.

Stella Daily Zawistowski is a copywriter from Brooklyn, New York, and a self-proclaimed brainy meathead. As of this writing, her personal records include a 325-pound deadlift and a *New York Times* Sunday crossword solving time of 4 minutes, 33 seconds.

Guest Writers

Jelisa Castrodale is a North Carolina–based freelance writer who has covered travel, food, sport, and pop culture for *VICE, USA TODAY, MSN,* and NBC Sports. She is also a *Jeopardy!* champion, who probably needs to stop mentioning that in polite conversation. Right now, she is either listening to David Bowie records or obsessing about Liverpool Football Club.

Luciana Chavez is a freelance writer from California. The UCLA alumna covered two of the most infamous losing sports programs in recent history: the pre-second act Kansas City Royals for the *Sporting News* and pre-Cutcliffe Duke football for the *Raleigh News & Observer*. She otherwise spends her time fundraising for sports teams at her high school alma mater, and perfecting K-pop dance routines.

Paul S. Paquet is an Ottawa-based trivia writer whose career has taken him to just about every corner of the quizzing world: He has had trivia columns in national syndication and in *Reader's Digest*; he's written for Trivial Pursuit, Uncle John's Bathroom Reader, HQ, the World Quizzing Championship, the Canadian quiz show *Instant Cash*, and many more. Paul is also the founder of the Trivia Hall of Fame, to which he was elected in 2018.

Neal Pollack is the editor in chief of *Book and Film Globe*, and a three-time *Jeopardy!* champion. The author of ten semi-bestselling books of fiction and nonfiction, and thousands of articles of great merit in every English-language publication except *The New Yorker*, he lives in Austin, Texas.

Kara Spak is a recovering newspaper reporter who spent more than fifteen years covering everything from crime to clowns. A five-time *Jeopardy!* champion, Kara kicked off her game show career by taking home a fax machine and dining room set on a 1997 episode of *The Price Is Right*. She lives with her family in Chicago.

Andrew Wineke is a writer, a reader, a basher of thumbs, a walker of dogs, and a teller of truths, great and small (but mostly small). He lives with his family outside of Seattle.

Index

Poop. *See* Crap
Porky Pig, 32–33, 206
Potato turds, 79
Power naps of gods, 223
Prince Edward Island, 167–68
Psychedelia, 61, 126
Pulitzer, Joseph, 151
Pulitzer, Lilly, 120
Pumpkin spice, 83–84
Puppidog-Water for the Face, 100

Quantum physics, 203–4

Rabies, 50
Radio station, suing, 81–82
Rage, Stevie, 58
Ramsay, Jack, 51
Ranch dressing, 99–100
Reality competition, 30–31
"Rebel Girl," 111
Red herring, 87–88
Reefs, 146, 179–80
Rendell, Ed, 54
Richter, Hieronymous Theodor, 71
Riggs, Bobby, 63
Rinsta, 35
Ripken, Billy, 140
Ripken, Cal, Jr., 140
Roberts, Jake "The Snake," 59
Robin, Christopher, 221–22
Robinson, Frank, 140
Robots
    on moon, 178
    of Philip K. Dick, 219–20
    starfish-killing robot, 180
    underwater robot, 180
Rockefeller, John D., Jr., 163–64

Rockettes, 163–64
Rojas, Henry, 51–52
Romance, bicameral, 162
Roosevelt, Eleanor, 164
Roosevelt, Franklin D., 45, 143
Roosevelt, Teddy, 132, 143
Rose Bowl game, 64–65
Rothafel, S.L. "Roxy," 163
Rowling, J.K., 229–30
Russia
    shadiness of, 115
    meat gels of, 31
    Nora Ephron and, 228
    stamp collecting and, 228
Ruth, George "Babe," 139
Ruzzo Reiss von Plauen, Prince
    Heinrich, 94

Sadness bowls, 89
Salad dressing, 99–100
Santa Claus, 166, 181–82
Santa Maria, 173–74
Sardines, 87–88
Sausages, 91–92
Schultz, Howard, 127–28
Schurz, Carl, 151–52
Schwarzenegger, Arnold, 219–20
Scuba-industrial complex, 179
Seashells, booby-trapped, 146
Self-coup, 106
Semordnilap, 212
Sex hair, 119
Shakespeare, William, ass of, 99,
    215–16
Shaw, Caroline, 162
The Shawshank Redemption, 28–29
Shit. *See* Crap

About the Editor

As chief editor of Geeks Who Drink since 2010, **Christopher D. Short** has read, looked at, listened to, written, and/or rewritten some 200,000 distinct pieces of trivia—and those are just the ones he was *paid* to. To date, he owns the record for least money earned by a six-time *Jeopardy!* winner (but still occasionally insists on being called Superchamp). He sings and writes church music in Crawfordsville, Indiana, where he lives with his wife, Jessica; his son, Maxwell; and a pitifully small dog named Paolo.